THE PURPOSE OF PASSION

The
PURPOSE
of PASSION

Dante's Epic Vision of Romantic Love

Kurt Bruner and Jim Ware

SALT**RIVER**®

An Imprint of Tyndale House Publishers, Inc.
Carol Stream, Illinois

Visit Tyndale's exciting Web site at www.tyndale.com.

TYNDALE is a registered trademark of Tyndale House Publishers, Inc.

SaltRiver and the SaltRiver logo are registered trademarks of Tyndale House Publishers, Inc.

The Purpose of Passion: Dante's Epic Vision of Romantic Love

Designed by Ron Kaufmann

Published in association with the literary agency of MacGregor Literary, 2373 NW 185th Avenue, Suite 165, Hillsboro, OR 97124.

Library of Congress Cataloging-in-Publication Data

Bruner, Kurt D.
   The purpose of passion : Dante's epic vision for romantic love / Kurt Bruner and Jim Ware.
      p. cm.
   Includes bibliographical references (p.   ).
   ISBN 978-1-4143-2059-5 (sc)
      1. Love—Religious aspects—Christianity. 2. Man-woman relationships—Religious aspects—Christianity. 3. Dante Alighieri, 1265-1321. Divina commedia. 4. Love in literature. 5. God (Christianity)—Worship and love. I. Ware, Jim. II. Title.
   BV4639.B84 2010
      241'.6765—dc22   2010029265

To our beloved wives, Joni and Olivia

TABLE OF CONTENTS

INTRODUCTION

Love's Divergent Paths

If we want to know what's most sacred in this world,
all we need do is look for what is most violently profaned.

—

Christopher West, *Theology of the Body for Beginners*

QUICK, NAME YOUR favorite romantic movie.

Got it? Now describe the best scene—the one you antici-
pate each time you watch. Depending upon your age, likely
choices include

Pride and Prejudice when the antagonism between Elizabeth
and Mr. Darcy melts as he anxiously confesses that
she has "bewitched me body and soul—I love, I love,
I love you";

Sleepless in Seattle when Tom Hanks takes Meg Ryan's hand
atop the Empire State Building as his matchmaker son
flashes that satisfied grin;

Titanic when Kate Winslet sloshes her way through the
frigid seawater-filled lower deck to reach Leonardo
DiCaprio, or when they embrace in the face of certain
death as the massive ship plunges downward;

My Big Fat Greek Wedding when John Corbett tells Nia
Vardalos, "When I met you I came alive!" (That line
is reminiscent of Tony's in the *West Side Story*, who
comes alive after meeting Maria, the girl whose name
became "the most beautiful sound I ever heard. . . .

Say it loud and there's music playing, say it soft and it's almost like praying.")[1]

Some consider the popularity of such stories a sign that our culture is overrun with lovesick adolescents rather than levelheaded grown-ups. They hit the pause button on their documentaries long enough to accuse those renting such films of being silly romantics trying to escape reality.

I beg to differ. I don't think we are trying to escape reality. We are trying to connect with it.

Since Adam's first double take at Eve, romantic love has been humanity's universal theme and most pined-after longing. And for good reason. More than any other experience in life, it reveals the purpose and ignites the passion of what it means to be fully human, fully alive.

Ask anyone who has ever had their timid smile returned by that special boy or girl across a crowded room.

Ask the guy who musters up the courage to hope, to call, to ask. Watch him leap for joy as she accepts, and see how long it takes him to lose that giddy grin.

Ask the girl who had lost hope of ever being asked for a date, yet suddenly finds herself holding hands with a man who considers her the loveliest woman on earth.

Or ask the husband and wife marveling at the tiny fingers of their newborn child, weeping as the joy of life rewards their intimate union.

They know.

We all know.

Hopeful Romantics

I knew the day I met a girl named Olivia, the woman who has been my bride these past twenty-five years. I've known on the days better became worse and back again. I've known in those moments she takes my breath away before we enter intimate bliss. She is my Maria, my Meg Ryan, Julia Roberts, Kate Winslet, and the rest all rolled into one wonderful package. She is also, as I was amazed to discover, my Beatrice—a woman who inspired the "script" all of our favorite romantic movies follow.

That story, written by a fourteenth-century romantic, is titled *The Divine Comedy*. As we will discover, a better title might have been *I Just Met a Girl Named Beatrice*. The script's author—just like Tom Hanks, Hugh Grant, Leonardo DiCaprio, and the rest of us—got swept up into a romantic journey that led him, and his readers, to a marriage made in heaven—literally. And that journey started with a single glance across a crowded room.

It turns out that the person best suited to guide us down lover's lane was an Italian. No surprise there. But he also ranks among the most influential Christian writers of all time. His name was Dante Alighieri. Yes, *that* Dante. You may have been forced to read his works during high school or college. You might recall his frightening portrayal of the afterlife. But don't let his fame for *The Inferno* fool you. Despite his knack for imagining hellish torments, Dante's signature theme was not the horrors of eternal damnation but the hope of romantic love. While he did describe how "the lust of the flesh" can destroy immortal souls, his more dominant emphasis was how a childhood crush can lead us to the very gates of heaven. Whether we find damnation or hope depends upon the choices we make along the way—a theme central to Dante's life and work.

The Scriptures tell us that God is love (1 John 4:8). So as those created in God's image, we are hardwired for a love that finds its source and aim in Him. We fully live when we fully love. And we fully love when we, like Christ, give ourselves away.

More on that later. For now, it is enough to recognize love as central to what it means to be human. The *imago dei* (image of God) was created male and female, two halves of a whole. That's why Love's magnetic force irresistibly and incessantly draws us toward that special someone who can become our completing opposite, our other half.

This idea is woven into the fabric of every Christian tradition. The late John Paul II, for example, said that "man becomes the image of God not so much in the moment of solitude as in the moment of communion."[2] Why? Because, as the catechism explains, "God who created man out of love calls him to love—the fundamental and innate vocation of every human being. For man is created in the image and likeness of God who is himself love. Since God created man and woman, their mutual love becomes an image of the absolute and unfailing love with which God loves man."[3]

The Scriptures are filled with marital imagery, describing Israel as God's wife and the church as Christ's bride. Protestant believers routinely celebrate the spiritual significance of romantic love, which is reflected in the opening words of the traditional wedding ceremony: "Dearly beloved, we are gathered together here in the sight of God . . . to join together this Man and this Woman in holy Matrimony; which is an honorable estate, instituted of God, *signifying unto us the mystical union that is between Christ and his Church*."[4]

Our attraction to one another is intended to yank us out of self-focused isolation into the kind of intimacy that reflects God's communion with His beloved. With us. That's why the desire for romantic union is imprinted on, programmed into, and seeded within our very souls. It's the reason we yearn to meet and marry that special someone.

Whether we find true love or ache from its absence, whether we treat sex as a gift or a game, our love life drives us toward or away from God. The forks encountered along love's path literally lead to heaven's highest joys or hell's deepest miseries, a dream come true or a living nightmare. That's why the headlines of history, art, pop culture, and family photos all shout a common truth: romantic love defines our existence—for better or worse.

Better or Worse

Walking love's path is a risky business. From the first step to the last, we navigate confusing emotions and competing impulses that tempt us this way or that. Each fork in the road presents a new challenge, rendering even Cupid's advice less than helpful. The journey of romantic love confronts us with varied choices, each pregnant with positive and negative possibilities.

Maybe that's why the Italian word Dante used for love (*amore*) suggests potentiality—like a seed that could sprout beautifully heavenward or twist and gnarl into a hideous mockery of its intended form. *Amore* might become a splendid flower that inspires or a creeping vine that strangles. It all depends upon how we tend love's soil.

- An admiring glance at her beauty or his stature can fan the flame of affection or fuel the inferno of lust, viewing the desired one as a person to love or an object to use.
- Your answer to that invitation to coffee could be a baby step toward lifelong love or a door slammed on any possibility of romance.

- A dinner date can become the foundation of lasting respect or the occasion for a hasty fling that leaves an aftertaste of guilt and shame.
- Every marital spat offers an opportunity to strengthen the relationship by humbly backing down or to dismantle it by flinging biting words and throwing defensive tantrums.

Deep down, we know our love choices carry more significance than meets the eye, as if something mysterious were working in us and on us. We know that each choice can move us closer to or further from the place we yearn to be and the person we hope to become.

Unsatisfied Yearning

The forks along Jonathan's path surfaced a deep yearning he could never fully satisfy. Once or twice he touched around the edges of God's design. But he always found himself choosing the downward slope leading away from joy.

In high school, Jonathan dated his "soul mate" and dreamed of settling down to raise a family together. But the girl's father had a different idea, forcing them to break off the relationship. Jonathan felt cut off from his "happily ever after" destiny. He forgot his heartache, thanks to other willing partners. Despite a religious upbringing that condemned promiscuity, Jonathan had urges and needs that girls seemed willing to satisfy. He eagerly accepted their generous offers.

In his late twenties, Jonathan fell in love with another woman. To his nervous delight, she became pregnant. At first, the thought of being a dad scared him to death. His own father had been an irresponsible jerk, and Jonathan hated the idea of following in his absent footsteps. So he resolved to break the cycle. His girlfriend and child would give Jonathan a purpose greater than himself, he thought, an opportunity to grow up, commit, and accept the responsibilities of manhood.

But things didn't work out as he had hoped. When the relationship deteriorated, Jonathan—like his father—abandoned the "family" to become a long-distance dad. Over the next few decades, he tracked his child's growth through the occasional photograph and infrequent letters. Lingering sorrow consumed his life. Tasting around the edges of God's design for love didn't satisfy; it couldn't make him feel whole or complete.

I'll never forget the call when we learned Jonathan had reached the bottom of the downward slope, ending his own life while wallowing in regret over what might have been. His death was a heartbreaking reminder that some of love's choices drag us toward the inferno.

Unimagined Bliss

Alicia's mom and dad divorced shortly before her birth— the inevitable fallout of an abusive and angry relationship. So along with her five siblings, Alicia lived in the shadow of abandonment by a man who chose the bottle over his wife and children.

Girls like Alicia are described as being particularly vulnerable to illicit male advances. Little girls need to feel like Daddy's little princess or they may try to fill the void through "acceptance" by lust-driven boys. Nonetheless, Alicia consistently chose the upward path.

High school boys made advances. Flattering? Yes. Tempting? Sometimes. But Alicia knew that she wanted God's best—something that would require patience and self-control.

During college several guys tried to woo Alicia. And while she enjoyed their company, none made her heart skip a beat.

And then one day, she spotted a young man walking across the campus who gave her pause. She glanced his way. He glanced hers. They talked for hours and hours about nothing and everything. When he asked her out on a date, she felt a new excitement—an irresistible draw—a magnetic pull.

Both Alicia and the young man believed that sexual purity before marriage would intensify the beauty and joy of sexual intimacy in marriage. So despite the thrill of each other's touch, they maintained healthy boundaries—considering their relationship a gift from and to their God, something they should protect and save, not waste or trivialize.

By the night of their wedding, Alicia was eager to give herself fully to the man who had treated her with such respect throughout their dating years. During the ceremony, she felt like a cherished princess. After the ceremony, during their honeymoon, and for many years thereafter, both enjoyed unimagined bliss.

Unlawful Indulgence

A lust-consumed man stares at a computer monitor surfing for images he knows it's shameful to enjoy. But he can't help himself; he's irresistibly drawn—no, addicted—to the female form. With each click of the mouse, he pulls up another image that he hopes will satisfy his unquenchable thirst. He can feel his manhood being undermined, his dignity diminished. So he pauses in momentary regret, reaching for the virtue and self-discipline he once possessed. Just as quickly, however, he turns back to the screen to find the next object of his insatiable desire.

A tearful runaway takes a long shower, trying to wash away the shame she feels after her first illicit encounter. Be it the abuse of rape or voluntary promiscuity, the loss of sexual innocence makes a person feel dirty, violated, ashamed. But that same girl will have a very different reaction after a year of prostitution. A cold stare tells you her heart is resigned to the shame that now defines her existence. A seductive glance suggests an acquired taste for erotic indiscretions. Dark shadows under her eyes and deep facial lines invade the soft, graceful beauty she once possessed. And loud, brazen laughter overtakes the gentle, pretty smile that was so charming just twelve months earlier.

When any of us is first introduced to the illicit pleasures of sin, there is a sick feeling in the pit of our stomachs. Our innocence has been violated—raped by a villain, seduced by an adulterous lover. We are, at first, ashamed. But before long, we forget what innocence is like and begin to prefer our fallen state.

The sad reality of defective love is that it drives us to crave that which should make us cry. The human race has been living in bondage to sin for so long that we cannot even remember the thrilling excitement and passion found in purity. Nor do we remember the intended object of our deepest longings. So we celebrate our addictions, viewing them as keys of liberation rather than chains of enslavement.

Such is the far-too-common reality of fallen humanity. The enticement and enslavement of sin pulls us deeper into the abyss of self-gratification. C. S. Lewis described this abyss as "an ever increasing craving for an ever diminishing pleasure."[5] Along the way we lose sight of who and what we were made to be. We adopt habits more suited to animals than to children of God. In the worst cases, the virus of one person's unlawful indulgence becomes the shameful abuse of another. The beautiful picture of our deepest aspirations becomes violently profaned.

Unexpected Redemption

Susan's innocence was stolen at a very early age. A trusted father figure used her preadolescent body to selfishly empty his passions. And so her virginity, that priceless gift intended for her future husband, became the discarded object of another man's lust. And as the story too often goes, she was similarly abused by several other men after that. Throughout her teen and young adult years, Susan tried satisfying desires awakened too early through one illicit relationship after another.

Susan later encountered the gospel of Jesus Christ—launching her into a new day in which "old things are passed away; behold, all things are become new" (2 Corinthians 5:17, KJV). Before long she met and married a Christian man who treated her like a lady rather than an object. But her past exploits kept her enslaved to an identity of shame and regret that robbed their relationship of the kind of playful intimacy that purity allows. The memories of past encounters left disfiguring scars on the masterpiece their union might otherwise have reflected. She felt, in a word, dirty.

As a child, Susan was wrongly shoved down a pathway of shame. Confronting her own forks in the road, she later made choices that further diminished her capacity for marital joy. But as she discovered, God is in the business of repairing what is broken, restoring what is taken, and redeeming what has been corrupted. Including lost innocence.

Over the years, Susan made choices that gradually released her from the bondage of her past. She found a measure of freedom by forgiving her abuser. She felt the cleansing power of grace by acknowledging and confessing years of self-abuse. She dedicated herself to giving the man she married uninhibited devotion—and by extension, a taste of the kind of love every person yearns to experience.

The stories are endless. Every person ever born has a tale to tell. For better or worse, choices made along love's path define our existence.

Properly positioned, magnets unite. They draw together unaided as two halves of a single whole. The same is true in romantic love. Properly focused, romantic love draws us toward completion. How? By inviting us to place someone else at the center of our universe. Defective love moves a person down the wrong path by focusing on "me." It flips the magnet around, so to speak, turning its uniting potential into a separating force.

No wonder Jesus said that we find our life only when we give it away. He was calling us to redirect love's focus from self-satisfaction to self-sacrifice.

Guided Tour

So what about your love life? How can you nurture its seed into blossoming flowers rather than life-strangling vines? How does a thrilling encounter with that mysterious stranger suggest falling in love with the God of all mystery? Our quest to answer such questions drew us into a surprising place—a fictional world imagined by a man who, as much as anyone in history, understood the all-encompassing meaning of *amore*.

In the past, Jim Ware and I have partnered to provide readers a scene-by-scene tour through such great book series as *The Lord of the Rings* and *The Chronicles of Narnia*. In this volume, we turn to the works of a man who inspired the writings of J. R. R. Tolkien and C. S. Lewis and helped frame their understanding of the gospel itself. In fact, my favorite books by C. S. Lewis, including *The Great Divorce*, *The Chronicles of Narnia*, and *The Screwtape Letters*, were profoundly shaped by *The Divine Comedy*.

To be honest, I did not always associate Dante with romance. But he, perhaps more than any other writer in history, connects the dots between the ups, downs, highs, and lows of human romance and the mountains, valleys, slopes, and ravines of humanity's spiritual quest. In my case he transformed the scenes of my relationship with Olivia into an icon of God's romance with humanity. That's why we recommend Dante as the best guide to discovering the purpose of passion.

Dante considered romantic love *the central theme* of human existence—both in this life and beyond. That's why his journey, like ours, begins with a seemingly silly boyhood crush in a bustling Italian village. That crush later hurls Dante into a spellbinding adventure through the underworld of *Inferno*, a purifying trek up Mount *Purgatory*, and the ultimate bliss of *Paradise*.

As we accompany our guide through these strange, imaginative worlds, we will encounter profound and sometimes troubling insights into the mysterious purpose of romantic love. It is a purpose rooted in the gospel of Jesus Christ, namely, to draw men and women into the arms of their ultimate suitor, God Himself.

Before our first stop we offer a quick overview of the route we intend to travel. The three sections of this book reflect the chronology of Dante's writings—starting with "Love Kindled"—a look at how and why romantic love invades our unsuspecting lives.

We draw these scenes from *La Vita Nuova* (*The New Life*), a book Dante wrote years before tackling his masterwork, *The Divine Comedy*.

Our second section ("Love Gone Astray") is based upon Dante's most famous work, *Inferno*. Here we discover the tragic consequences of defective love—including the downward pathways often chosen on love's perilous path.

Finally, in part three we will join Dante on the upward climb back toward love's intended destiny (*Purgatory*) and ascend toward "Love Fulfilled" where we discover the true and eternal object of our affections (*Paradise*).

Each reflection opens with a creative retelling of a scene from *The New Life* or *The Divine Comedy* from which we connect the dots between human romance and the epic love story between God and His people. At the end of each of the three sections, we will take a break from our journey in order to reflect upon how Dante's encounters inform our own. These "Getting Personal" sections pose penetrating questions intended to drive home Dante's sometimes lofty ideals by making them practical in the real-life experience of dating, marriage, and Christian devotion.

We should note that Dante's works are imaginative fiction. They were not intended to be works of theology or doctrine, and they contain ideas of the afterlife that are clearly speculative. While some Christian traditions resonate with Dante's portrayal of Hell, Purgatory, and Paradise more than others, his fictionalized scenes should be understood as literary devices expressing a greater theme, not as dogmatic teaching.

With that, we begin our journey. May Dante's Romantic Vision ignite within you, as it has in us, a greater fire of godly passion—no matter where you find yourself on love's journey.

PART 1

Love Kindled

La Vita Nuova (The New Life)

Incipit vita nova.

———————

The new life begins.

—

LA VITA NUOVA, CHAPTER I, TRANS. MARK MUSA

CAPTIVE

FLORENCE IN THE YEAR 1283 was a bustling city of proud nobles and prosperous merchants: a multihued harlequin carnival of a town, where men in dark gowns and women in bright dresses hurried arm in arm through the narrow, winding streets; where tall houses of honey-colored stone lifted red-tiled roofs high above white marble fountains and beds of red geraniums; where black and gold pennants flew atop the square bell towers and painted placards swung creaking in the shadowed doorways of the shops; where, in the springtime of the year, fresh-faced boys and girls danced underneath a cloudless sky in the piazza, which was adorned with ribbons and flowers.

At such a time and on such a day, while leaning on a balustrade at the corner of the Via Tavolini and the Via de' Cerchi, Dante looked up and saw her coming. She was dressed all in white. So light was her step that she seemed

3

to float between her two matronly companions. At the sight
of her his heart stood still, for this was *Beatrice.* The same
Beatrice he had seen on another spring day when he was nine
and she was only eight years old. As she drew near, all the
color and pageantry of Florence faded from his view in the
light of her emerald eyes.

Instantly he was swept up into the memory of that
distant but unforgettable day. Again he saw her as he had
seen her then: a slim young girl in a blood-red dress, her
forehead smooth, her eyes bright, the daylight soft upon
her hair. Again he heard a voice that said, "Now your bliss
draws near!"

He trembled and swayed. He felt his mouth go dry. And
still she came, nearer every moment, more radiant and more
beautiful at every step. With a thrill of terror he realized that
she saw *him,* too—that she was, in fact, looking straight at
him, her eyes sparkling, the corners of her mouth turned
slightly upward, her head inclined modestly in his direction.
So close was she now that he could smell her perfume and
see the gold highlights in her hair. He backed away, stam-
mering. And then, as she passed, she turned and spoke:

"*Buon pomeriggio,*" she said. "Good day to you, Dante."

It was the ninth hour; and though the afternoon was
only half gone, the air grew dark around him. Blindly Dante
stumbled from the place. Heedless of everyone and everything,
he wandered through the streets until at last he found the door
to his house and staggered into his room.

There he fell senseless upon the bed, his head filled with
fevered visions. A fiery cloud. A woman wrapped in red cloth.
A man of "fearsome aspect" with a flaming object in his hand.
"I am Love!" said the man. "Behold your heart!" Dante awoke
in a cold sweat.

Outside his window the sky was dark. A single star shone above the roofs of the neighboring houses. He rose, blundered against the desk, groped for a pen, and wrote:

A ciascun' alma presa e gentil core . . .
To every captive soul and loving heart . . .[1]

It was the beginning of a new chapter. His life would never be the same.

Boy meets girl. Boy falls in love. Boy's world is turned upside down and inside out.

It's the theme of a thousand poems, the refrain of a million popular songs. It's the commonest thread in the entire tapestry of human experience, the most familiar, most frequently repeated tale in the world. But it may also be the most mysterious and most poorly understood—at least where its *eternal* implications are concerned.

The first time we meet Dante Alighieri—in *La Vita Nuova* (*The New Life*), the earliest of his extant literary works—he is a boy in love. When next we see him, in the third chapter of the same book, he is a *young man* in love. By the time he crosses our path again, at the entrance to Hell in the opening cantos of the *Inferno*, he is in many ways a very different person: older, wiser, sadder. But he is still an incurable romantic. For wherever this man goes and whatever he does, he is always the devoted servant of Love.

This is where we have to begin if we want to understand the author of *The Divine Comedy*. The first thing we need to know about Dante is that he lived his entire life as the slave and captive of Love. He was Love's secretary, Love's stenographer. He was a writer who, "when Love inspires me, takes careful note and then, gives form to what he dictates in my heart."[2] Dante's poetry, the highest and most perfect expression of the "sweet new style" of fourteenth-century Italian verse, represents the pinnacle and fullest flowering of the medieval tradition of courtly romance. Romantic love was the creed of his existence, the theme of his thoughts.

It all started on a street corner in Florence. It began in the simplest way such a story can possibly begin: with a girl. Dante was smitten with Beatrice at first sight. The instant he saw her coming, something exploded in his soul. It was a fireworks display to rival anything ever sparked between Lancelot and Guinevere, Tristan and Isolde, Fred Astaire and Ginger Rogers, or Brad Pitt and Angelina Jolie. The result was a spiritual "stupor" that produced within his nine-year-old brain an all-consuming "sense of reverence and a desire to know more."[3] So overwhelming was the experience that he forever after regarded it as the occasion of his *rebirth*—the point at which his "new life" had begun.[4]

Such is the potency of Romantic Love. The Bible is no stranger to the power of this intoxicating fire. What Dante felt upon seeing Beatrice for the first time is the same feeling King Solomon experienced when he looked at his Shulamite bride and cried,

> You have ravished my heart,
> My sister, my spouse;
> You have ravished my heart
> With one look of your eyes. (Song of Solomon 4:9)

The explosive nature of romantic love shows up even in modern popular culture. This was the same sweet cataclysm, for example, that shook young Beaver Cleaver's world when he fell under the spell of Miss Canfield, his second-grade teacher. Love compelled Beaver to do things he never would have done under any other circumstances. He passed out spelling books. He stayed after school cleaning chalkboards and beating out erasers. He endured the teasing and ridicule of his friends. When his older brother, Wally, confessed that he, too, had once fallen for an "older woman," Beaver asked the obvious question: "Did you ever get over her?" "No," was Wally's reply. And Beaver, with a solemn nod, said, "I don't think I'll ever get over Miss Canfield either."[5]

In a certain sense, we can be sure that he never did. For Love, as Dante discovered in his terrible dream, is an exacting and unrelenting taskmaster. Love, by its very nature, makes grandiose claims of everlasting permanence. Love, as Solomon understood, is the most formidable force in the world. It irreversibly changes the human heart. It binds its victims with gentle cords and bands of sweet affection (Hosea 11:4). Its grip is as tenacious as the grip of death itself (Song of Solomon 8:6). Once it lays hold of you, it never lets go (Hosea 11:8). It follows you through all your ways, seeks you through joy and pain, and obliges you to live with open hands and heart. It takes possession of your entire life.

Like Dante, the apostle Paul was a slave and captive of Love. He did the things he did because he was *compelled* or *constrained* by the Love of Jesus (2 Corinthians 5:14). Though a leader of almost unparalleled authority in the early church, Paul consistently referred to himself as a "servant" and a "prisoner" of Christ (Ephesians 3:1), the same Christ who loved him and gave His life for him

(Galatians 2:20). He said that Love is the one great obligation laid upon all who sincerely desire to follow the King of kings (Romans 13:8).

Is it fair to speak of *this* love and Dante's infatuation for Beatrice in the same breath? If we follow our poet far enough, we will learn that his answer to this question is *yes*. More than that, we will discover that this yes is central to the meaning of his poetry. For *eros* (romantic love) and *agape* ("charity" or divine love),[6] while distinct in many ways, are not, after all, two different plants of two different species. They are, in fact, branches of one and the same tree—a tree whose roots go down to the well at the heart of the world. To put it another way, love is Love wherever you find it. The magnetism of the girl in the red dress is just a reflection, an emanation, an extension of the Power "that moves the sun and the other stars."[7]

Like most young romantics, Dante had no idea what he was getting into when he fell for Beatrice Portinari. But then how was he to know? Who could have told him that his romantic inclinations might turn out to be his salvation? That his devotion to the young lady with the stunning emerald eyes would eventually lead him down through the depths of hell, up the steep sides of the holy mountain, and out into the crystal spheres of the heavens beyond?

But we're getting ahead of our story.

REFLECTION
Love is a life-changing force.

BEREFT

Di necessitade convene che la gentilissima Beatrice alcuna volta si muoia.

———

Of necessity, the most noble Beatrice will have to die some day.

—

La Vita Nuova, chapter XXIII; trans. Stanley Appelbaum

DANTE WAS WRITING another poem when the news reached him, a poem birthed out of the trials and sorrows of love. He meant it as a celebration of his lady's beauty and virtue, a tribute to the terrible sweetness of the subjection in which she held him. It was cast in the form of an ode, and it began with the words "So long has Love held me."[1]

As indeed it had. For more than fifteen years he had been prisoner to her charms. He had lived for the sound of her voice. He had drawn all his sustenance from her greetings and smiles. And when, as the result of a misunderstanding, those greetings had been temporarily withdrawn, he had fallen into a pit of deep despair.

In the heart of that darkness, Love had appeared to him a second time: not as a fearsome tyrant, but as a silent visitor, weeping by the side of Dante's bed.

"Why do you weep?" asked the poet in his dream, and

Love answered, "Because I am like the center of a circle. From my perspective, all points on the circumference are equally distant. But with you it is not so."

Since that day Dante had labored to build his world around a core of selfless Love. He had praised his lady without expectation of advantage or gain. He had repented his ill-conceived plan to conceal his devotion by feigning interest in another. He had come close to saying about Beatrice what had never been said of any woman: "Heaven has no lack but the lack of her. The saints and angels call for her presence."

So it was that, in continuing obedience to these vows, he had come to his writing table once again. There he sat, quill in hand, striving to express in words how *Amore* had led his heart, soul, and spirit abroad in search of the ultimate Good:

> *They go forth, they call upon my lady,*
> *They ask her to give me more salvation.*[2]

Salvation. A daring choice of words. But even as he penned it, a knock came at the door. On the step stood his friend Guido Cavalcanti, pale and solemn.

"What is it, Guido?" Dante asked, a strange sense of foreboding descending upon him like a sudden evening chill.

Guido's hand was on his arm. "I'm sorry to be the one to tell you, my friend. It's Beatrice. Heaven called her home. Not an hour ago."

The face of Guido disappeared in a numbing fog. When next he became aware of his surroundings, Dante was back at the table, crumpling the unfinished poem in his fist. His eye fell upon a copy of the Scriptures that lay open to the book of Lamentations.

"How lonely sits the city that was full of people!" Catching up the volume, he shouted the words, flinging them out against the blank white wall. "How lonely! How like a widow is she!"

Blackness overcame him. He dropped the book and fell forward, covering his head with his hands.

It was long before he came to his senses again.

"'Tis better to have loved and lost," wrote Tennyson, "than never to have loved at all."[3] The English novelist Samuel Butler, in a more cynical frame of mind, introduced a slight alteration to Tennyson's dictum: "'Tis better to have loved and lost," he said, "than never to have *lost* at all."[4] Dante's work demonstrates that *both* of them were right.

If God *is* love (1 John 4:8), and if love is therefore the soul and center of the universe, it follows that a life without love is a poor and paltry thing. What may be less apparent to the unobservant eye is that love without the anguish of loss can be equally threadbare and shallow. Bereft of bereavement, love easily falls short of its divinely appointed goal. In this case, the popular maxim "no pain, no gain" is eminently applicable and inescapably true.

There's a good reason for this. In a perfect universe, human life would be a matter of uninterrupted progress from one degree of bliss and fulfillment to the next: a delightful stroll along a gently sloping upward path. This, of course, is not our situation. We are fallen people living in a fallen world. Having rejected our Maker's original program in favor of the god of self, we must now make our way forward according to a different set of principles.

The key words here are *redemption* and *resurrection*. Under the new system, we rise to the celestial realms, not by way of our own efforts, but by being *lifted up* by the grace of God (Ephesians 2:8-9). It's a glorious plan, but there's a catch, for *resurrection* naturally presupposes death, and there can be no *redemption* where there has not first been some kind of loss. Such is the topsy-turvy economy of God's Kingdom.

The full account of Dante's early romance with Beatrice is long and complicated; you'll find the details in *La Vita Nuova* (*The New Life*). For our present purposes, the important thing to notice is this: just at the point when Dante's passion was approaching its zenith, its object was cruelly snatched away. Just when his devotion to his lady was at its height, Beatrice suddenly fell sick and died. It was a devastating blow for the sensitive young poet, a trauma from which he never fully recovered. But it was not the end of his love for the lady with the shining green eyes. In a very real and profoundly important way, it was only the beginning. And thereby hangs the balance of our tale.

Author Sheldon Vanauken has a remarkably similar story to tell. He and his young wife, Davy, were deeply in love. Romance caught up with them early in life. It led them on an exciting and eventful journey from youth to adulthood, from courtship to matrimony, from rural Virginia to the University of Oxford, from unbelief to a deeply satisfying faith in Christ. From the beginning they guarded their love jealously, surrounding it with what Vanauken called a "Shining Barrier" of protection against the eroding influences of the outside world. But just when it seemed that the intensity of their oneness was as sweet as it could possibly be, Davy came down with a strangely persistent and mysterious virus. Death claimed her before the year was out.

Why did it have to happen? From a certain perspective, that's a question that cannot be answered this side of eternity.

But on another level Vanauken came to believe that Davy, in some mysterious and profoundly spiritual way, had offered up her life on his behalf—that she had died "for the fulfilment of [his] soul."[5]

It was C. S. Lewis, Van's friend and mentor since his Oxford days, who helped the young widower arrive at this painful yet enlightening conclusion. The older and wiser Lewis, gifted with keen insight and genuine compassion for his grieving friend, recognized that there had been something too "*us*-centered" about Van and Davy's romance. "One way or another," Lewis gently suggested, "the thing had to die."[6] This was the theme of a letter he wrote to Vanauken soon after Davy's death:

> I sometimes wonder whether bereavement is not, at bottom, the easiest and least perilous of the ways in which men lose the happiness of youthful love. For I believe it must *always* be lost in some way: every merely natural love has to be crucified before it can achieve resurrection and the happy *old* couples have come through a difficult death and re-birth. But far more have missed the re-birth.[7]

This, in a nutshell, is the story of Dante and Beatrice. As Dante attempts to show in his *Divine Comedy*, love has the potential to lead the lover to the highest of all heights. But even the seed of love, when sown in the hearts and minds of *fallen* lovers, is unlikely to grow aright until it is watered with the rain of sorrow. It need not be the sorrow of physical death. It may consist simply in the realization that the true meaning of romantic devotion emerges only when beauty fades and the flame of youthful passion flickers.[8] The real work of redemption begins with the birth pangs of suffering and doubt. "Unless a grain of wheat falls into the ground and dies, it remains alone; but if it dies, it produces much grain" (John 12:24).

It is, of course, frighteningly easy to stray from this narrow and rigorous path. All too often we fail to grasp the lessons that loss and hardship are meant to teach us. We become bitter rather than better. As Lewis observed, we encounter death but miss the experience of rebirth.

Apparently this was the case with Dante. Though he never tells us exactly *how* it happened, he does make it clear that, in some important way, he bungled the test that came to him in the form of Beatrice's death. Instead of learning how "[her] buried flesh was meant to guide [him] in another way,"[9] he wandered from the track, took the wrong fork in the road, and wound up in a tangled forest of darkness and despair.

That's where we find him when *The Divine Comedy* begins.

REFLECTION
Loss reveals the essence of Love.

BETRAYAL

Onde io, accorgendomi del mio travagliare, levai li occhi
per vedere se altri mi vedesse. Allora vidi una gentile donna
giovane e bella molto, la quale da una finestra mi riguardava.

Remembering my suffering, I raised my eyes to see whether
anyone was looking at me. Then I saw a kindly young lady,
very beautiful, who was looking at me from a window.

—

La Vita Nuova, chapter XXXV; trans. Stanley Appelbaum

TIME PASSED. DAYS TURNED into weeks and weeks into
months. At length an entire year had passed since the death
of Beatrice. And still the pain of Dante's loss—the loss of his
earthbound angel, his bright and vibrant vision of something
like the glory of God walking along the streets of Florence—
did not subside.

Under its relentless chafing, the fabric of his life grew
threadbare and pale. His existence became a monotonous suc-
cession of waking and sleeping; of going and coming; of labor,
study, prayer, and official business. He staggered through this
patchwork of dark and light like a man hypnotized or under
a spell, waiting vaguely for someone to shake him and wake
him from the imprisonment of his dream. It was while he was
walking along the street in this state that he saw the lady in
the window.

Her face was as beautiful as it was warm and compassionate. The sky over the piazza was not so softly blue as the eyes that looked down upon him from out of that lace-trimmed casement above the street. Those eyes *saw* him—he knew they did—and so filled were they with sympathy for his abject condition that he could not help but pity himself the more. For an instant he stood paralyzed on the pavement. Then the sash fell and the face was withdrawn from his sight.

From that moment forward the memory of the face possessed him. Again and again he returned to it in his thoughts, finding comfort in its softly rounded lines and tender blush. Day after day he loitered in the street beneath the window, hoping for another glimpse of those eyes. And he wrote sonnets that gave form to his vision: "My eyes beheld all the compassion" and "amorous pallor and expressions of pity."

Then one afternoon it hit him. A question struck him like a thunderbolt from a cloudless sky. What in fact had he been making of this lady in the window? Had he perhaps begun to think of her as a person he liked too well? Was it conceivable that she had usurped the place of the blessed Beatrice in his affections, that her kindness and beauty had eclipsed the vision that first possessed him in the house of the Portinaris during the spring of his tenth year? It was a devastating possibility. Overwhelmed with sudden shame, he went home to his darkened house and fell down in a stupor.

That night she came to him in his dreams: not the lady in the window, nor yet the dazzling young woman in white who had rendered him speechless on the Via Tavolini, but the eight-year-old girl in the blood-red dress: the original Beatrice, the primal power of Love. She said nothing but only gazed upon him sadly, then slowly turned and faded from his view. As on that night so long ago, he awoke in a trembling sweat.

"What have I been thinking?" he cried aloud. "How on earth could I have allowed these desires to possess me for so many days in direct contradiction to the better inducements of my mind?" He knew now what he had to do: he must forsake the lady in the window. He must turn again and reassert his loyalty to his first love.

Burying his face in his pillow, he gave way to his tears.

The Divine Comedy begins with Dante lost and wandering in a dark forest. We have suggested that Dante never precisely defines the waywardness that eventually led him into the dismal wood before Hell's gate. But this doesn't mean that he leaves his readers completely in the dark on this point. He actually gives us several important hints as to the nature of his failure to pass the test of bereavement.

The most noteworthy of these occurs in *La Vita Nuova*, just eight chapters after the death of Beatrice. Here he tells us how, within a year or so of that cataclysmic event, he allowed his head to be turned by the glances of a beautiful young woman sitting at a window. In retrospect, he came to see this "shameful" infatuation as a flat-out betrayal of his former love. Convicted of his error, he repented and reaffirmed his devotion to his lost lady. And as proof of his faithfulness, he resolved to exalt her memory by saying of her "that which has never yet been said of any woman,"[1] a pledge he fulfilled in the writing of *The Divine Comedy*.

In and of itself, this episode seems straightforward enough. But things get messy when we remember that, around this same time, Dante actually *married* another woman—Gemma Donati.[2] If his fascination with the lady in the window was worthy of censure, what are we to think of his marriage? Was it yet another instance of unfaithfulness to *Amore*?

This would be a strange idea, of course, since neither the New Testament nor the teachings of the church hold Christian couples to a rule of *postmortem* fidelity. Furthermore, Beatrice had never been Dante's wife.[3] She wasn't even his "lover" in any conventionally accepted sense of the term. As a matter of fact, *La Vita Nuova* gives us scant reason to suppose that she and Dante ever exchanged more than a few sentences during the entire course of their earthly acquaintance!

If she was neither wife nor paramour, what *was* Beatrice Portinari to Dante Alighieri? There is only one way to answer this question. To Dante, Beatrice represents the *meaning* of the experience of "falling in love." She is his "imaginative formation" of that most astonishing quality or state of human consciousness.[4] She is, in short, his embodiment of the Romantic Vision. And as such, she demands her poet's exclusive and undying loyalty.

If you are young and in love—or if you are older and can remember what it was like to be in that condition for the first time—you will know what that Vision and that experience are all about. You will understand that falling in love is something deeper, more primal, and far more all-encompassing than mere infatuation or sexual desire. It is *ecstasy* in the truest sense of the word: a sense of "standing outside" yourself. It involves astonishment and surrender. It is bliss and terror at the approach of another person who suddenly appears before you in "a blaze of beauty and goodness."[5] It means losing and finding your identity in someone else.

Dante described this frame of mind by saying, "If anyone had asked me for anything at such times, my reply would have been merely 'Love.'"[6] Observes Charles Williams,

He was so highly moved that he was, for the moment,
in a state of complete goodwill, complete *caritas*
towards everyone. . . . He becomes for one moment
in his soul that perfection which he has observed in
Beatrice. . . . Love, charity, agape, was for the moment
inevitable. . . . But it was to be a long time before he
could himself become that state permanently. . . . The
rest of Dante's work is a pattern of the Way.[7]

It was to the all-consuming potency and significance of
that one blissfully self-forgetful, other-centered moment that
the poet could have and should have remained faithful when
the body of Beatrice was moldering in the grave. Instead, he
allowed his attention to be deflected from the center of the
circle. In the midst of his misery, he glanced around to see
if anyone was looking at *him*. And it was precisely at that
instant that his eyes were drawn to the lady in the window.

Interestingly enough, Dante later made the claim that
this lady had never been a flesh-and-blood woman at all.
In book II of the *Convivio*, he suggests that she was in fact
none other than the Lady Philosophy, implying that he
had sought consolation for his loss *not* in a new romantic
preoccupation but rather in "authors, sciences, and books."
The sincerity of his statement is open to doubt. But it does
indicate (among other things) that he somehow viewed such
studies as yet another betrayal of the Vision, another deviation from the middle path.

Here again we are faced with an apparent inconsistency.
For just as Dante married Gemma Donati without any
apparent compunction or regret, so he remained a zealous
disciple of wisdom and knowledge to the end of his days
despite his assertion that devotion to the Lady Philosophy

entailed some kind of disloyalty to the memory of Beatrice. What does this mean?

Once more the solution has to be sought in the nature of the Romantic Vision. That Vision, as we have seen, is all about transport and wonder. It is at heart an imaginative journey into what Charles Williams calls the process of "in-othering": the melting and melding of the self with another self. This is precisely what merely intellectual pursuits can never give us. For as Dorothy Sayers observes, "It is the weakness of Humanism [by which she means human philosophy] to fall short in the imagination of ecstasy."[8]

Dante will later insist that genuine love is always rational. It treasures knowledge and understanding and remains in constant conversation with the mind. But for the time being he wants us to recognize that the intellect is wholly inadequate in and of itself. For all its good points, it lacks the outwardly propelling power of the Romantic Vision. The enlightenment it offers is too introspective, too inwardly focused. Even in its best moments it is rather like a beautiful lady whose favoring glances only inspire a man to posture and preen; for knowledge, as the apostle Paul points out, is notoriously self-inflating (1 Corinthians 8:1).

Romance, on the other hand, is like a door to another world. It is a path to adventure, a portal to discovery, an unpredictable but far more excellent way. For all these reasons it demands that we cling to its visionary promise with unswerving determination and hope—for its goal is nothing less than our complete transformation.

REFLECTION

Love is loyalty to the Vision of the outward bound.

GETTING PERSONAL
When Love Is Kindled

SEAT BELTS HAVE BEEN BUCKLED, hats removed, security bars locked and checked. You feel initial movement and obediently "keep your hands and arms inside the vehicle." Moments later, the clank and clatter of pulley chains engage beneath your feet. The sounds tighten your stomach, intensify your grip, and stiffen your body. Leaning back against the headrest, you feel yourself ascending ever more slowly until those in front of you reach and conquer the peak. Too late for second-guessing. There can be no turning back. The only thing left to do is throw up your hands and prepare to scream!

Dante Alighieri, like those screaming in the front car, offers advance warning to those anticipating the wild-and-crazy journey of love's roller coaster. While we may not see what lies ahead or fully grasp the details of his experience, the squeals of terror and delight let us know that something frightening and thrilling is about to happen to us. Clearly, this will not be a gentle "tunnel of love" journey.

The ride of romantic love should post more clearly marked signs alerting us to what we can expect.

Warning: This ride is not for the faint of heart. It can cause extreme stress due to unexpected twists and turns, dramatic climbs and drops, and sudden changes in direction. Expect some or all of the following:

Sudden loss of breath at the sight of her or thought of him
Dizzy spells in conjunction with giddy infatuation
Petty spats and major arguments requiring the courage to apologize and forgive
A possible broken heart caused by breakup, unfaithfulness, or death
Radical transformation of your body, soul, and spirit

Proceed at your own risk!

Of course, we don't actually stand in line or volunteer for the journey of romantic love. It is thrust upon us—catching us off guard and by surprise. Like young Dante, we enter the experience naive and ill-prepared. As his encounter with the lovely Beatrice and the disturbing images of the lady in the window show, *Amore* draws us into a mysterious adventure that disturbs our sleep and invades our dreams. It is unpredictable, unscripted, and sometimes unfair. There are no clear-cut rules or step-by-step instructions. So we heed the screams of a poet rather than craft a detailed plan.

Dante's early encounters give cause for each of us to ask ourselves a few penetrating questions that can help us steer the ship of love. Romantic winds may fill our sails without warning, but we can make choices that harness their power toward our intended destiny.

Question 1: Have you opened yourself to the thrilling risks and life-altering demands of romantic love?

Don't answer too quickly. Let's first unpack the question.

Even if you are married or in a serious relationship, don't assume you've opened yourself to the formational changes love demands. Many do not. You see, every one of us is bent toward self-satisfaction, not self-sacrifice. That's why we tend to preserve the status quo, maintain our boundaries, and defend our rights. You've heard the lines, maybe even spoken them:

> "I'm enjoying my freedom right now. There's no hurry."
> "He's a nice guy, but I don't want to settle. I'm holding out for my soul mate."
> "I'll back down and apologize if she does first."

The truth of the matter is that we don't want to make ourselves vulnerable. And yet becoming vulnerable to another person is essential to the romantic journey as well as our spiritual maturation.

Like a deer in heaven's headlights, sooner or later we will be forced to go one way or the other. We can continue to isolate and insulate ourselves, or we can risk ascending the path of love. And the risk is enormous. Just ask the One who embodies obedience to love's ultimate call.

> Let this mind be in you which was also in Christ Jesus, who . . . humbled Himself and became obedient to the point of death, even the death of the cross. (Philippians 2:5-6, 8)

The easy part of love is thinking about another person. We do that naturally, sometimes even selfishly. The hard part is thinking less of oneself. Nothing is more unnatural or selfless. That's why we are commanded to "let nothing be done through selfish ambition or conceit, but in lowliness of mind let each esteem others better than himself. Let each of you look out not only for his own interests, but also for the interests of others" (Philippians 2:3-4).

The seed of love can only blossom into its intended flower when the lover embraces the last thing he or she wants—humility. That's because the crucible of conformity to the image of Christ is not personal, solitary contemplation. It is rather the gritty, grinding, daily reality of one person rubbing another the wrong way. It happens little by little as we lay aside our own interests, give up our selfish desires, and decide to serve the person we've been given to love. A person, at times, we may not even like.

Of course, love is much more than dying to self and cheerless humility. It has a bright side—a very, very bright side. Romantic intimacy is one of God's most thrilling, awe-inspiring gifts. Yes, it requires us to become vulnerable by laying our lives on the line. But remember what Jesus said. Unless a seed dies, it remains alone (John 12:24).

Love, and the risky sacrifices it requires, brings a quality of life available only to those who muster enough courage to strap on seat belts, remove their hats, and raise their arms for a great ride!

Have you opened yourself to love's risks and rewards? Nothing in this life will challenge, cheer, or change you more.

QUESTION 2: ARE YOU WILLING TO ENDURE THE PAIN OF LOSS IN ORDER TO KNOW THE JOY OF REDEMPTION?

Dante lost the girl of his dreams. She died before her time, before he could begin to enjoy the life he dreamed possible with her and perhaps *only* her. What does his experience suggest for our journey?

First, we will lose the person we risk loving. Not *might* lose them. It is a certainty. And it will hurt, badly.

For some, the loss comes before the first date; the short brunette in love with a guy who likes tall blondes; the guy who musters enough courage to ask out his dream girl only to find out she hopes they can "be good friends." The pain of losing cuts deep, even if we lose what we never really had.

For others, the pain comes through death after decades of bliss, or through divorce after years of fighting. No matter when, how, or why—losing someone we've loved is one of life's most painful experiences.

In the 1993 film *Shadowlands*, Anthony Hopkins portrays C. S. Lewis (a.k.a. Jack) during the years he fell in love with and married Joy Gresham—a feisty American single mom played by actress Debra Winger. In real life, Joy died of a painful form of cancer only a few short years after their betrothal. Her illness remained a dark cloud hovering over their relationship from the start. Both knew that their time together would be short. And yet, knowing full well how hard their separation would be, they feasted on the joys and pleasures of romantic love.

As the credits roll at the end of the movie, viewers wipe away the tears while reflecting on the questions posed by Jack's experience. Why was Joy taken so soon? Why didn't God give them more time together? Was the pleasure of love worth the pain of loss?

Earlier in the story, Jack and Joy discuss these very questions—anticipating the day she will lose her battle with cancer.

"It's not going to last, Jack." Joy says it first, forcing the discussion they've both avoided since her diagnosis.

"We shouldn't think about that now," he responds, unwilling to spoil an otherwise happy moment.

"I'm going to die," she presses forward.

"I'll manage somehow. Don't worry about me."

"I think it can be better than that," Joy says. "I think it can be better than just managing." She goes on to explain that the pain Jack will feel when he loses her is mysteriously wed to the happiness he feels while he has her.

"That's the deal," she says.

Dante would agree. We must not merely attempt to "manage" when confronted with loss. We must see it as an essential scene in love's redemptive tale.

The thirsty man eagerly drinks.

The shivering cold warm their feet by the fire.

In similar manner, those who've tasted the heartache of loss welcome the comfort of restoration. And those who have known the grief of death yearn for the joy of resurrection.

Losing the object of our affections—whether due to separation, rejection, death, or divorce—gives us the unwelcome opportunity to experience God's restorative grace. Unwelcome, but essential. That's because something must cause us to shift our focus from the gift—no matter how praiseworthy—to the Giver. The apostle Paul expresses this change in focus in one of his letters:

> But what things were gain to me, these I have counted loss for Christ. Yet indeed I also count all things loss

for the excellence of the knowledge of Christ Jesus my
Lord, for whom I have suffered the loss of all things,
and count them as rubbish, that I may gain Christ.
(Philippians 3:7-8)

Whether you are considering a relationship, struggling
to keep one together, or anticipating the death of a lifelong
partner, the journey of romance will, at some point, bring the
painful sorrow of loss. And, if you are ready to receive it, the
beautiful grace of redemption.

At the midpoint of his life, still mulling over the lost potential
of true love, Dante finds himself leaving the ordinary scenes
of this life to experience the astonishing wonders of the next.
We join him standing in a dark wood just before he encounters the dehumanizing scenes of a place called the Inferno (the
Italian word for *Hell*)—a place filled with those whose love
went dreadfully astray.

PART 2

Love Gone Astray

Inferno

*Tanto giù cadde, che tutti argomenti
a la salute sua eran già corti,
fuor che mostrargli le perdute genti.*

—

To such depths did he sink that, finally,
there was no other way to save his soul
except to have him see the Damned in Hell.

—

PURGATORY, CANTO XXX, 136–138; TRANS. MARK MUSA

ANOTHER WAY

A te convien tenere altro viaggio . . .
se vuo' campar d'esto loco selvaggio.

But you must journey down another road . . .
if ever you hope to leave this wilderness.

—

Inferno, canto I, 91, 93; trans. Mark Musa

GOOD FRIDAY, 1300. Dante woke alone in a gloomy wood. He had no idea where he was or how long he had slept. So deep was the darkness that he could not even tell if it was day or night. Only one thing was clear to him: *he had lost the way.*

Struggling to his feet, he brushed the crumbs of rotting leaves from his cloak and peered into the murk. In the distance a faint gray smudge appeared between the black boles of the trees. *A light.* He slashed through the bracken, watching as the gray swelled to blue and the blue slowly resolved itself into a patchwork of violet, yellow, and green.

At the edge of the wood he leaned, panting, against the trunk of a massive oak and looked out. Beyond the eaves of the forest rose a high green hill, crowned with the red-gold rays of the rising sun. The first gentle slopes of the Delectable Mountain! A swell of hope rose in his breast.

Gathering his strength, he set off up the grassy hillside.

But halfway to the top a sharp feline scream stopped him cold. There was a flash of teeth and fur. He dodged and fell, then scrambled to his feet. Not three yards in front of him crouched a spotted leopard, sleek and long flanked, muscles tensed, ready to spring. Slowly Dante backed away, three measured steps, then turned to run.

That's when he saw the lion. Squarely in his path it sat, its yellow eyes following his every move. He stopped, trembling, then slowly edged his way up and over a rocky rib of the hill. *Safe at last*, he thought.

But on the other side of the ridge stood a mossy boulder, and atop the boulder squatted a huge she-wolf. Her tongue lolled hungrily from her dripping maw. The hatred in her fierce red eyes struck him with all the force of a well-aimed blow. *Trapped.* The game was up. He dropped to the ground and stared.

"So quickly discouraged and thrown off course?" said someone behind him.

Dante turned to see a tall, long-faced man in a Roman toga. On his head he wore a chaplet of laurel leaves. An ink-horn and writing case dangled at his belt.

"Virgil?" Dante stammered in disbelief. "The *poet* Virgil? My model, my mentor, my inspiration! And looking just as I've always pictured you! But how—?"

The old Roman raised a hand. "I was *sent*. From beyond the grave. By One who wants to see you reach the summit of that hill as much as you do. But you cannot climb it by this path. Such opponents are too strong for the likes of you."

"Then how?"

The poet smiled. "The Hound is coming," he said. "*He* will deal with the leopard, the lion, and the wolf. Meanwhile, you must follow me on another road. Down into the deep parts of the earth, through the lowest galleries of Hell. Down, down, down, until you come at last to the place where *down is up*." He paused. "Are you willing?"

Dante nodded.

"Then come with me," said the poet, extending his hand. "Follow me, and I will take you there."

"I'm sorry, but it's over. Can't we be just friends?"

If you've ever heard those terrible words, you know exactly what they mean. They spell the end of the Romantic Vision. They're the seal on the tomb of Love. They're the gateway to every lover's personal hell.

That hell is especially deep and dark when it's a hell of your own making; when you know in your heart of hearts that the dream didn't simply die of its own accord, but that, somehow or other, you strangled it yourself; when the beasts of guilt and shame and self stand between you and any possibility of regaining what's been lost. The only thing worse than a shattered romance is the consciousness that you are the shatterer.

That dismal, desperate feeling is what hell is all about. If you've known it, you've sunk about as low as a man or woman can sink. The loss of love, as Dante learned, is perhaps the most painful and dehumanizing of all human losses. But great as it is, it isn't necessarily the end of the line. For as our poet was also destined to discover, the gateway to hell lies strangely near the threshold of heaven.

The road to Paradise runs straight through the Inferno. This is one of the central messages of *The Divine Comedy*, Dante's masterful sequel to *La Vita Nuova*. It may be the most important message of all. That's because Dante, who allowed the death of his own dream to deflect him from Love's true path, understood what it means to be blameworthy, helpless, and utterly *lost*. More importantly, he grasped what this lostness implies for the destitute lover who aches to regain the Vision and follow it to its Source.

"Why not climb up this blissful mountain here, the beginning and the source of all man's joy?"[1] asks the poet Virgil, Dante's guide through the unseen realms, when he finds the pilgrim wandering in a dark and dismal wilderness. Why not indeed?

The answer to that question, which Virgil himself supplies only sixteen lines later, is as blunt as it can be. Dante cannot climb that hill. He cannot climb it because the road is closed. The inescapable, ever-present reality of his own faults, inadequacies, and sins, represented by the leopard, the lion, and the wolf, are blocking the way. In his own strength he will never overcome these formidable opponents. "This beast," says Virgil, referring to the she-wolf, "allows no soul to succeed along her path."[2]

Here is a spiritual principle that we dare not overlook. When our first parents fell from grace, the world changed its shape. To borrow an image from Tolkien's mythology, all roads were *bent* at that decisive juncture. As a result, the straight path to Paradise is no longer open. The way through the Garden has been forever closed.

Something similar can be said with respect to the loss of the Romantic Vision. When the girl of your dreams says, "Can't we be just friends?" you suddenly find yourself on the wrong side of an impassable abyss. All in an instant, the flame is snuffed. It was like that for Dante when Beatrice died. Her smiles, her sighs, her gentle greetings—everything passed away beyond the chasm that separates the living from the dead. Dante was barred from that particular pathway to bliss. For him, nothing remained but a barren wilderness and a pit of despair.

What's a poor pilgrim to do at a time like this? Virgil knows: the traveler must find the faith and courage to follow another road.

There's nothing easy about that road. It's a path of downward rather than upward mobility. As we've already seen, it's the way of death—of suffering, sorrow, and self-denial. Everything about it defies common sense. It goes against the grain of human understanding. It's a scandal, an offense to human reason. After all, how can one expect to ascend the heavens by sinking into the bowels of the earth?

The answer to this riddle, as Virgil assures his bewildered pupil, lies in a wondrous promise: an astonishing message of unforeseen hope. A Deliverer is coming. *He* will remove the barriers and bring the paradoxes to life. *He* will destroy the leopard, the lion, and the wolf. *He* will unbend the world and restore the Romantic Vision. *He* will engineer a highway to Heaven by boring a passage straight through the slag pits of Hell.

Only one Hero is capable of accomplishing such a feat. Only one can defeat the beasts of self-centeredness, infiltrate the stronghold of Hades, and proclaim liberty to captive souls (Luke 4:18-19; 1 Peter 3:18-19). We know who He is and we know His name. It is Jesus Christ, the Hound of Heaven, the celestial Trailblazer. He is the King of Love, and He redeems all merely human loves by drawing them into the circle of the divine. He is the One who has "descended into the lower parts of the earth" (Ephesians 4:9) in order to light a pathway through the darkness.

This is why Hell stands so near to the doorstep of Heaven: because only the desperate are likely to bank their hopes on the scandal of a Savior. Only the bent are prepared to endure the pains of the straightening process. Only the lost are ready and willing to be found.

This is why Dante cannot be saved until he is given a chance to "see the Damned in Hell"[3]—and why we cannot follow Him to the celestial heights until we descend with Him into the depths of twisted despair.

REFLECTION

What goes up must first go down.

CHAIN OF LOVE

Perchè ardire e franchezza non hai
poscia che tai tre donne benedette
curan di te ne la corte del cielo . . . ?

Why art thou not delivered, eager, bold,
When three such blessed Ladies of their grace
Care in the court of Heaven for thy plight . . . ?
—

Inferno, canto II, 123–125; trans. Laurence Binyon

THE PATH FELL steeply between banks of crumbling rock, more like a ravine than a road. Far out ahead the bald crown of Virgil bobbed up and down, up and down, while the staff of Virgil rose and fell with a predictable, rhythmic *crunch*. Dante followed at a distance, trembling, sweating, and panting like a dog though the trek was all downhill.

"Master," he said breathlessly when they stopped for a moment to rest, "why were you sent to me? Why was *I* chosen to make this journey?"

Virgil raised an eyebrow. "Afraid, are you? Well. That's only natural. But as to why I was sent—it was because of the *ladies*."

Dante stared.

"One in particular," said the old Roman with a wry smile. "But she didn't act alone. Oh, no. You're a highly favored fellow, you are. You're on the receiving end of a veritable *chain* of feminine grace. It seems the grandest and most gracious lady of all has been rather concerned about you. She called on Lucia for help. Lucia went straight to Beatrice. And Beatrice pulled *me* into the mix. Came all the way to Limbo to fetch me. Yes, I *did* say Beatrice. Don't look so shocked. And don't imagine that I can't understand," he added with a wink. "She's quite stunning. As soon as I saw her I said, 'Command me, my Lady.' What else could I say?"

In a few moments they were off again, Dante trailing behind the ancient poet with a feeling of lightness in his heart, his head filled with visions of her shining emerald eyes. *Beatrice!* he said to himself, almost skipping over a pile of shale that lay shattered in the road. *She sent for me! She cares for me!* He felt as if he could face a whole pack of ravenous she-wolves for the chance of seeing her radiant smile again.

That's when a shadow fell across his path. He looked up to find that they had stepped beneath a huge black opening in the rock. Beyond it lay a darkness of roiling mist. Over its mouth ran an inscription etched in letters six inches deep:

> *Here lies the entrance to the City of Woe.*
> *No hope remains to those who through its portals go.*[1]

Dante felt his heart drop to the pit of his stomach. He clung to Virgil's sleeve, mute with dread. A blast of frigid air swept over them from out of the cavern's depths.

Then, as he watched, his guide bent down and peered into the murk. Slowly Virgil's furrowed brow grew smooth. His frown relaxed. The corner of his mouth curled upward in a half smile. He turned and touched his companion's hand.

"Don't worry," he said softly. "I can see it! The chain I

told you about! Even in this darkness its links glitter with heaven's light. It's quite long—long enough to reach even *you*. Courage, then! From this point forward your motto is *trust*. Cling to hope as you would to life itself."

He gripped his staff and led the way forward.

It's a terrible thing to be caught between the devil and the deep blue sea, to look up and see uncertainty looming in the distance while despair bears down hard from behind, to doubt your ability to move forward while knowing that there can be no turning back. If you've ever found yourself in such a dilemma—trapped between fear and desperate hope—you'll understand how Dante felt as he stood trembling at Virgil's elbow in the shadow of Hell's gate.

In that awful moment our hero was confronted with two contradictory messages, two pieces of advice so diametrically opposed that they seemed to cancel each other out. *Abandon all hope*, said the first—not an unreasonable suggestion under the circumstances. *Hold fast to trust*, countered the second—a word of comfort and encouragement made all the more enticing by the fact that it came straight from the mouth of Virgil, Dante's divinely appointed mentor and guide. Which of the two was the pilgrim to embrace? How was he to know which way to turn?

The answer takes us back to the theme of *Amore*—the redemptive power of Romantic Love—and straight to the heart of *The Divine Comedy*'s central message.

In scanning the blackness beyond the infernal gate, Virgil perceives something that Dante himself has missed: a slender cord, strung lightly between the two opposing poles of despair and determination; a silver chain bridging the gap between dreaded judgment and hoped-for mercy; an unforeseen third ingredient, capable of blending fear and longing in a miraculous elixir of life. The name of that cord, that chain, that ingredient, is *Love*. And the strands, the links, the elements of which it is composed are the souls of the saints and believers—in this case, Mary, Lucia, and Beatrice. In this moment of darkness, Dante receives assurance that these blessed ladies are monitoring his progress from their exalted place in the heavenly realm.

There's an important message here for all of us: we must not expect to succeed in the Christian life *alone*. That life is ruled and shaped from beginning to end by Love. And Love—even the Romantic Love of Dante and Beatrice—is never a purely private and personal affair. When a man and woman meet and melt with mutual passion, they are bonded not merely to one another but to the larger human family.

"When I found the one I love," says Solomon's bride in the Song of Songs, "I held him and would not let him go, until I had brought him to the house of my mother, and into the chamber of her who conceived me" (Song of Solomon 3:4). Lovers *as lovers* are always part of a larger family. They inevitably become links in an eternal chain. Whether they know it or not, their *Amore* brings them into relationship with an ever-expanding number of significant others. Ultimately, it ties them to *all* who climb the upward road that leads to the Author of Love.

To put it another way, Love is a matter of *community*. By God's love we are grafted into the olive tree of the commonwealth of faith (Romans 11:17) and become members of the body of Christ (1 Corinthians 12:27). We are united with Him, spirit to Spirit, and with one another in the bond of charity. This is what believers mean when they confess their faith in "the communion of saints,"[2] a transcendent fellowship that spans the centuries, encircles the globe, and unites heaven and earth. Within this communion we stand shoulder to shoulder with *all* men and women, living or dead, who belong to the Lord of Love: "for none of us lives to himself, and no one dies to himself" (Romans 14:7).

That's why the writer of Hebrews can assure us that our spiritual progress, like Dante's, is being watched by a "so great a cloud of witnesses." Above our heads gather all the holy pilgrims who have traveled the celestial road before us. They huddle around and cheer us on as we "run with endurance the race that is set before us" (Hebrews 12:1). Out in front of the crowd, in full view of the heavenly grandstand, stands the Lord Jesus Himself, our Chief Cheerleader and Advocate with the Father (1 John 2:1). *He* is the One who intercedes for us day and night in the court of Heaven (Romans 8:34; Hebrews 7:25; 9:24), procuring for believers the confidence we need to "come boldly to the throne of grace" (Hebrews 4:16).

It's no accident that, in Dante's case, this communion of saints, this chain of Love, is composed specifically of *ladies*. We'd be untrue to our author if we failed to underscore this aspect of his imagery. Like the lovely women of Florence, to whom Dante, the incurable romantic, had *always* looked for consolation in affairs of the heart,[3] and like Matilda, Leah, and Rachel, who will later speed him on his way to the top of Mount Purgatory,[4] Mary, Lucia, and Beatrice are here to remind us of a vital spiritual truth: that Love itself is a Lady.

God's love is the feminine blush at the heart of the universe. His shekinah glory, a feminine noun in the original Hebrew, is a female presence that longs to be joined in passionate union with the human soul, just as it was joined with the soul of Moses at the top of Mount Sinai.[5] It's a yearning tenderness at the center of all things. It says to the sinner,

"How can I give you up?" It pleads with the prodigal, "How can I let you go?" (Hosea 11:8, NLT). This Divine Love holds the promise that, in the end, compassion will triumph over judgment, that mercy and truth must finally be one, that righteousness and peace are destined to meet in a holy kiss (Psalm 85:10). She is always a lady of the highest degree to all who devote themselves unfailingly to her service.

This is the Love that reaches down and delivers Dante as he stands quaking in his boots at the gate of Hell. It is neither an esoteric theological concept nor a piece of dry and dusty doctrine. It is, on the contrary, someone with an extremely familiar face—a quintessentially *human* face—the face of a dark-haired, green-eyed Florentine girl. It's the Love of God the Father reflected and expressed in the tenderness of a woman. It's a shimmering silver chain of feminine affection and motherly longing. And it stretches itself to him, link by precious link, even through the darkly burning haze of the Inferno.

REFLECTION

God's love is a cosmic family affair.

OFF-CENTER

Amor condusse noi ad una morte.

Love led the two of us to a single death.

—

Inferno, canto V, 106; trans. Stanley Appelbaum

DOWN, DOWN THEY WENT, following the black and broken road deep into the heart of the earth, Virgil leaning heavily on his staff, Dante supporting himself against broken boulders and slipping over loose stones and gravel. The unspeakable journey had begun in earnest. Already they had passed the Vestibule of Hell, where the diffident and irresolute linger in eternal indecision, and the Circle of Limbo, where virtuous pagans languish in endless shadows. Even the court of Minos, serpent-tailed gatekeeper of the underworld, lay behind them. Ahead the path sloped down to a cliff at the edge of a howling darkness.

"We've reached the Second Circle!" Virgil cried, cupping one hand round his mouth and pointing over the precipice. Dante pulled his cloak up over his head and squinted into the blackness. Gradually he became aware of shapes hurtling past the cliff's face on the fury of the storm: naked souls, mainly in pairs, soaring and dipping and swirling like leaves in a cyclone.

"Who are they?"

"Devotees of luxury in love," shouted Virgil. "Those who saw no harm in a little extracurricular dalliance. Look! There's Semiramis. Do you see? And Cleopatra. And Paris and Helen. And Tristan and Isolde. All connoisseurs of sweet diversion."

Dante stood transfixed, gazing into the abyss. And as he did so, a familiar face suddenly leapt at him out of the maelstrom.

"Francesca!" he cried, gripping his guide by the arm. "It's Francesca da Rimini! And Paolo! May I—," he hesitated. "Is it permitted—?"

"By all means," said the old Roman. "That's why we came. Call them! Charge them to stop in the name of love! They won't be able to resist *that*!"

There were tears in Dante's eyes as the pair of lovers turned aside and clung to the cliff in obedience to his cry. "Francesca!" he said. "I know your face! I have heard your story! You were one of those I celebrated in my poetry. A noble lady, a gentle heart, quick to kindle with love." He would have touched her hand, but fear and awe restrained him.

"Love," she said, her eyes downcast and demure. "Yes. Love is sweet. Sweet upon the lips. Sweet to the taste. Love led us here," she added, casting a sidewise glance at her pale companion. "And so here we are. Together. Forever."

"But—why?" Dante stammered. "How could Love's journey end *here*?"

She sighed. "We were in the garden. I was reading to him. It was the tale of Lancelot and Guinevere, how they kissed for the very first time. When I looked up, his eyes were fixed upon me, but not on my face. His lips, full and richly curved, were parted ever so slightly. I put the book down. We never finished the story."

Dante looked from one to the other. Paolo wept silently. Francesca sighed again.

"My husband found us, you see. We were pierced through. Together. Pierced by love." She smiled at him sadly. Then, taking Paolo by the hand, she let go of the cliff. The torrent of air swallowed them up and swept them away.

Dante felt the blood drain away from his face. His ears tingled. The world went black around him. And then he knew no more.

On September 4, 1962, after nine days of hurtling sunward at a rate of 25,420 miles per hour, the *Mariner 2* spacecraft was on course to *miss* its target—Venus, the planet of love—by a margin of 233,000 miles. The solution? Mission Control fired *Mariner's* fifty-pound-thrust rocket motor for a total of *twenty-seven seconds,* producing a mere fifty-nine-mile-per-hour decrease in velocity and an alteration in trajectory so slight that it would have been barely perceptible at the time. But by December 14 that small shift had brought *Mariner* to a point just 21,000 miles above the surface of Venus—well within the spacecraft's limited operational range. The moral of the story? Given time, an adjustment of one or two degrees can make a difference of 212,000 miles.

This is precisely the principle we see at work in the story of Francesca da Rimini and Paolo Malatesta, the ill-starred lovers Dante finds tossing on the winds of lust and desire in the Second Circle of Hell. It's one of the most famous and best-loved episodes in the entire *Divine Comedy,* often cited as an example of the poet's "tenderness"[1] toward romantically motivated sinners. On the surface it appears to present the adulterous pair (Francesca was the wife of Paolo's brother, Gianciotto) in a touchingly sympathetic light.[2] But a closer look reveals that Dante has a different reason for introducing them to us at this juncture in the narrative.

Here's the problem he wants us to ponder. Boy meets girl. Boy falls in love. "A noble awe and a noble curiosity come to life" in his soul.[3] It's all very wonderful and romantic and inspiring. But it raises a rather obvious question: *what happens next?* Paolo and Francesca are here to show us what *can* happen when Love is deflected—however slightly—from its true trajectory.

What exactly *was* the sin of Francesca da Rimini and Paolo Malatesta? A number of obvious possibilities come immediately to mind. Adultery. Sexual immorality. Forbidden love. Broken vows. All very serious transgressions in and of themselves. But in this instance there's a sense in which they have to be regarded as mere formalities—symptoms rather than the underlying disease.

The real problem here is the spiritual sickness Dante attributes to *all* the miserable souls who go whirling about on the storm of the Inferno's Second Circle. He refers to it as *lussuria*.[4] This Italian noun is usually translated as "lechery" or "lust," and it certainly includes these meanings in the present passage. But it also denotes something far subtler and more insidious.

In essence, *lussuria* is "luxury." It's "indulgence" or "self-yielding." It's that tiny shift in a person's attitude toward any object of devotion, be it lover, friend, social cause, spiritual truth, or God Himself, that transforms it, however imperceptibly, into a means to an end—generally a *selfish* end. It's the desire to touch and taste purely for the sweetness of the sensation, to linger in the moment for the moment's sake. It has less to do with the beloved than with what a person hopes he or she can *get* from the beloved. In the case of Francesca and Paolo, it was "the first tender, passionate, and half-excusable consent of the soul to sin."[5]

What does all this have to do with the hero of our story? What object lesson is Dante the pilgrim supposed to draw from the example of Paolo and Francesca? He gives us a clue in chapter 12 of *La Vita Nuova*. There, as we have already seen, he describes how, at a crucial moment in the development of his feelings for Beatrice, Love spoke to him in a dream. "I am like the fixed center of a circle," said Love. "But with you it is not so." Charles Williams comments:

> The alternative to being with Love at the center of the circle is to disorder the circumference for our own purposes. This—the perversion of the image—is in fact the sole subject of the *Inferno*.[6]

Dante's assignment, like that of any lover, was to find his place at the center of the circle. He was supposed to *become* the kind of Love that "does not seek its own" but rather "bears all things, believes all things, hopes all things, endures all things" for the sake of another (1 Corinthians 13:5, 7). Unfortunately, he failed. In some way he never fully explains, he fell prey to *lussuria*. His passion for Beatrice was deflected from its proper trajectory. Gradually, imperceptibly, he began to think of her primarily in terms of *himself*. Like Paolo and Francesca, he yielded to the temptation to turn a person into an object. As a result, he was put on a course to miss his original target by a million miles.

This, Williams suggests, is the whole reason Dante has to make his journey into the depths of Hell. In the Inferno he is shown exactly where this small change in orientation would have led him had it been left uncorrected. The wretched people he meets and the horrible scenes he witnesses on his way down to the center of the earth, like the visions granted to Scrooge on Christmas Eve, are pictures of what might have been had the rocket motor of Beatrice's untimely death never been fired. And Paolo and Francesca represent the first step down on that descending stairway to perdition.

Could Solomon have been thinking of this same small step when he warned his son to beware of the woman whose lips "drip [with] honey"?

> Her mouth is smoother than oil;
> But in the end she is bitter as wormwood,
> Sharp as a two-edged sword.
> Her feet go down to death,
> Her steps lay hold of hell. (Proverbs 5:3-5)

Such is the downward progression by which their love led Paolo and Francesca to a common death. It's a concept that won't sit well with some modern readers. "It can't be wrong when it feels so right," we like to say. "Passion is always its own justification." But as Charles Williams points out, "Those err who think that all love is in itself worthy of praise."[7] This, as we shall see, is one of the major themes of *The Divine Comedy*.

It's only fair to add that, according to Dante's imaginary hierarchy, the transgression of Francesca and Paolo turns out to be the least damnable and most understandable of all the offenses punished in the seven circles of Hell. In and of itself, their furtive, forbidden kiss is a relatively small and insignificant thing.

But it's still a step away from the center of the circle.

REFLECTION

Love your neighbor as—not for—yourself.

SURPRISE, SURPRISE!

E chinando la mano a la sua faccia,
rispuosi: «Siete voi qui, ser Brunetto?»

And, stooping down to bring my face near his,
I said: "What, you here, Ser Brunetto? you!"

—

Inferno, canto XV, 29–30; trans. Dorothy Sayers

LEAVING PAOLO AND FRANCESCA BEHIND, Virgil and Dante
pressed their relentless journey deeper into the bones of earth.
Down through the shivering rains of Hell's Third Circle they
descended, past the Gluttons wallowing in freezing mud.
Across the Fourth Circle they tramped, where Misers and
Spendthrifts roll dead weights from opposite ends of a circle,
forced always to turn the opposite way when they meet in
the middle. When the two travelers came to the Fifth Circle,
located along the spongy banks of the River Styx, they saw the
steaming swamps where the Wrathful rage. They watched the
bubbles burst on the surface of the slothful fens, evidence of
the Sullen submerged beneath the murky waters. Through the
gates of the City of Dis they entered the desolate wilds of the
Sixth Circle. Among the flaming tombs they heard the heretic
Farinata speak darkly of Dante's future.

At length they came to the Seventh Circle, where violence

of all kinds—against neighbors, against self, against nature and nature's God—served as its own worst punishment. As they emerged from the dismal Wood of the Suicides, where the souls of self-destroyers awaited their doom in the shape of dry trees, Virgil called a halt.

"Watch yourself, now," he said, shading his eyes and squinting out across the burning desert that lay beyond the fringe of trees. "You can be sure *they* will."

He pointed to the barren plain, where flakes of fire and brimstone rained down upon crowds of naked red souls, some of them dancing a miserable tarantella over the scorching sands, others crouching on their haunches or writhing on their bare backsides. From out of their midst a troop of harried-looking sinners ("Sodomites," Virgil whispered behind his hand) was moving up the torrid slope, their movements sharp and unnatural, their skinny necks stretched forward, their penetrating eyes fixed narrowly upon the two travelers. In a moment Dante found himself surrounded.

"How delicious!" said a voice behind him. "What a delightful treat!"

In the next moment he felt someone seize the skirt of his garment. He wheeled around and braced himself. Then he stopped short in dismay.

"Master Brunetto!" he exclaimed, unable to believe his eyes. He caught his breath and drew back. Then, tentatively, he reached out to touch the twisted face and scalded features. "Brunetto Latini! My old teacher! *Here?* But—?"

"Need you wonder why, my boy?" asked the shade with a grin. "Yet I trust you won't take it ill if I fall in behind for a few moments of . . . fellowship?"

"Take it ill?" Dante responded. "Why, I insist! How can I do less? You were my light in the darkness! The wisest, most educated man of your age! You taught me everything I know. You showed me what it means to live eternally. No one could have been more fatherly! No one more loving or kind! If you had any fault at all, it was that you loved me *too much*! How can I possibly repay you for all you've done?"

Brunetto frowned. "That much, at least, I can tell you. If you love me, then have a care. Watch your back! *They* will seek to devour you. Not *these* wretches—I speak of the perverted Florentines! Look to yourself! More I cannot say. Now farewell!"

Then away he went over the glittering sands, restless, sinewy, bare, and burnt. For a long while Dante stood gazing after him, thinking that he resembled nothing so much as a runner stripped for the race. At last he turned at the touch of Virgil's hand.

"Consider yourself forewarned," the Roman said. "Well-heeded is well-heard."

The writers of the *Pirates of the Caribbean* trilogy of films confidently assure us that it is possible to be both "a pirate *and* a good man."[1] In *The Divine Comedy* Dante learns that one can be a "good man" and also go to Hell.

This realization comes home with brutal force in the Third Circle of the Inferno, the Circle of Overindulgence, where Ciacco, a small-time glutton and drunkard, informed our hero that many "worthy men" and eminent public figures could only be found in the lowest pits of the underworld. Where was Tegghiaio Aldobrandini, Dante wanted to know, that brave and valiant knight? Where was Farinata degli Uberti, the wise Ghibelline leader who single-handedly saved the city of Florence from destruction after the disastrous battle of Montaperti? Where were Jacopo Rusticucci, Mosca dei Lamberti, and all those others who were "so bent on doing good"?[2] Ciacco knows. They are "with the blacker spirits below, dragged to the depth by other crimes abhorred."[3] Hell, it seems, is full of rude surprises.

Enter Brunetto Latini. It wouldn't be going too far to say that Brunetto is the best of the "good men" Dante finds languishing in the cellars of Perdition. Biographers are divided on the subject of his precise relationship to the author of the *Commedia*. Some think he was Dante's tutor. Others deny this, pointing out that he would have been about fifty years old at the time of the poet's birth. Still others propose that Latini may have been Dante's stepfather. The historical facts are far from clear.

One thing, however, is beyond doubt: Dante felt that he owed the older man an eternal debt of gratitude. If the young poet did not actually sit under Brunetto's teaching, he must certainly have drunk deeply from the well of Brunetto's writings—the *Tesoretto*, a work of allegorical poetry, and *Li Livres dou Trésor*, an encyclopedia of the knowledge of the day. In the *Inferno*, Dante addresses the venerable scholar with great respect, calling him "Ser Brunetto" and employing the formal Italian pronoun *voi* (you). He "speaks of and to him as he speaks of and to no-one else in Hell"[4]—with tenderness, affection, and admiration. "My mind is etched (and now my heart is pierced)," he declared, "with your kind image, loving and paternal. . . . I am so grateful, that while I breathe air my tongue shall speak the thanks which are your due."[5]

Why should this kind and fatherly figure—this man of wisdom, erudition, courtesy, and grace—be cast into Hell? It would be easy to resort to the obvious explanation. Brunetto was a Sodomite. He had violated nature through acts of homosexual perversion. But the case is by no means so simple. For if Latini shows us anything, it is that one can be both "a Sodomite *and* a good man." Unfortunately, he also demonstrated that a "good man" can be utterly lost. And *this* is a point that concerns us all.

Jesus often spoke on this theme. He warned us that the Kingdom of Heaven does not necessarily belong to the kind of people we might *expect* to find there. It is not the possession of great writers and doctors of theology, but of the spiritually poor, the meek, the mournful, and the weak (Matthew 5:3-5; 2 Corinthians 12:9-10). It's a topsy-turvy world where the first are last and the last first (Mark 10:31), where "tax collectors and harlots" go in ahead of respected religious leaders (Matthew 21:31), and where those who have preached to others stand a very real chance of being disqualified themselves (1 Corinthians 9:27). Heaven, like Hell, is a place full of shocking surprises.

That's because salvation is not a matter of totting up moral and spiritual pluses and minuses. It isn't about determining whether the sin of sodomy or the virtue of fatherly kindness deserves the greater weight in the scales of divine judgment. It's simply a question of *receiving* the gift of grace—in other words, of responding correctly to the romantic advances of God's redeeming Love.

We are forced to conclude that Ser Brunetto's chief deficiency, the fundamental flaw underlying his more patent sins, was in fact an offense against grace and Love. This is precisely how Dante understands it. In his view, Latini's interest in young male students is something more than a dirty little secret or a regrettable character flaw. It is, in fact, another example of *Love gone wrong*—a further step down the descending stairway of the distortion of the Romantic Vision.

This is why T. S. Eliot can say that "the case of Brunetto is parallel to that of Francesca . . . so admirable a soul, and so perverse."[6] This is why Charles Williams observes, "Brunetto is indeed the nearest to the shape of a damned Beatrice."[7] For if Paolo and Francesca's self-indulgence represents a subtle deviation away from the center of the circle, Brunetto's sodomy is a very sharp and definite turn in the wrong direction. It's a version of "love" in which *lussuria* dominates all, and the beloved almost ceases to exist except as a means of the lover's self-gratification.

Latini's brief discourse concludes with a word of warning. On the surface, it's a warning our pilgrim will hear many times during the course of his journey: a prophecy of his impending exile from the city of Florence. But in this particular context the words assume a deeper significance. As the dignified old scholar races off with the rest of the accursed crowd, we can almost hear him say:

> Let my example be a lesson to you: be careful of the sharp left turn! "Take heed, watch and pray" (Mark 13:33) lest you, too, be surprised. Be on guard against the perversion in your own heart—"the pestilence that walks in darkness" and "the destruction that lays waste at noonday" (Psalm 91:6). It's what you are becoming on the inside that counts. So stay on target. Respond in love to the Love that first loved you. Follow the star that appeared to you on that street corner in Florence so many years ago. And "see that you cleanse yourself of their ways."[8]

REFLECTION

Good enough is never good enough.

HIDDEN BEAST

Io avea una cordaa intorno cinta,
e con essa pensai alcuna volta
prender la lonza a la pelle dipinta.

Around my waist I had a cord as girdle,
and with it once I thought I should be able
to catch the leopard with the painted hide.

—

Inferno, canto XVI, 106–108; trans. Allen Mandelbaum

THE PLAIN OF SAND and fiery rain swept down to a rocky
precipice over which the waters of the three infernal rivers—
Acheron, Phlegethon, and Styx—tumbled together in a thun-
dering cascade. The two travelers trudged forward beneath
the barren trees, the roar of the water drawing nearer at every
step. Behind their backs the rasping voices of the Sodomites
continued to carp and whine, while on his right Dante was
vaguely aware of a group of Usurers who sat at the edge of
the Seventh Circle, swatting at the burning snowflakes as
people swat flies or mosquitoes. In the distance squatted the
Moneylenders, each one clinging desperately to a brightly
embroidered cash bag that hung from a strap about his naked
and peeling neck.

When they reached the cliff, Virgil stopped and laid a hand
on Dante's arm. "Now, then!" he shouted above the pounding

of the waterfall. "If we're to go any farther, I'll have to have your help. What's that you're wearing around your waist?"

Dante looked down at the rope belt with which he had girded his hooded gown. It was plain and rough, nothing but a length of braided hemp.

"It's just a cord, Master," he yelled back. "The humble belt of the Friars Minor. The monks use them to cinch up their plain brown robes. Haven't you ever seen one?"

"Give it to me," Virgil said briskly, holding out his hand.

"But I—"

"Sorry, no time!"

With fumbling fingers, Dante undid the cord, coiled it, and laid it across the old Roman's wrinkled palm. With that, Virgil reached back and hurled the piece of rope far out over the rocky rim. It hung there briefly in the air, twisting among the sunless drops of mist above the falls. Then it was gone, lost in the shadows below the cliff.

Together they leaned forward and peered over the edge. *What next?* Dante wondered uncomfortably, gathering the loose folds of his garment about him as the rushing of the waters pounded in his ears. The answer wasn't long in coming.

Something was swimming up to meet them from out of the shifting shades of gray beneath their feet: a shape uncannily like that of a diver rising to the surface of the sea, but horribly malformed and monstrous in size. Its face, as it emerged from the swirling fog, was that of a plain and honest man. But behind it trailed the loathsome coils of a multicolored serpent, bright with rainbow scales and tipped with a deadly two-pronged scorpion's tail. The beast drew near and grasped the cliff, leaning against the rocks with its furry forelimbs as a man rests on his arms at the edge of a pool.

Dante shrank from the apparition. "At one time," he confessed, "I had hoped to snare the spotted leopard with that rope."

Virgil laughed. "Well, it's a different sort of catch you've landed now. Meet Geryon—the face of Fraud itself! Now, don't be shy. Climb up on his back! Yes, I *am* serious! It's the only way to reach the last two circles!"

In our travels with Dante we have already discovered that it is possible to be a good man and still end up in Hell. It remains to be shown that the same can be said of the earnestly *religious* man—and that the deadly snares of deceptive religiosity lie dangerously close to the path of Romantic Love.

The concept of religion is a product of the classical civilization of Greece and Rome. Our English noun is taken directly from the Latin *religio*, a derivative of the verb *religo*, "to tie back, fasten up, bind fast." Religion, then, is a system of binding obligations. It's a matter of rules and regulations. It emphasizes outward forms and appearances, sometimes at the expense of inward realities. This is why the apostle Paul can say that religion—or, as he might call it, the "letter of the Law"—not only fails to save (Galatians 3:11) but actually *kills* the human soul (2 Corinthians 3:6).

The cord that Dante removed from his waist as he stood looking down into the lowest regions of Hell is more than a fitting image of the "binding" nature of religion. It may also indicate that Dante himself knew what it was like to fall prey to the temptations of the religious life. Referring to the dark years immediately following the death of Beatrice, biographer Paget Toynbee writes,

> Perhaps it was at this period that Dante . . . joined the
> Franciscan Order. This tradition is held by some to
> be confirmed by Dante's reference in the *Inferno* (xvi.
> 106–8) to the cord with which he was girt, the cord
> being one of the distinctive marks of the Franciscans,
> who were hence known as *Cordeliers.*[1]

We are not accustomed to think of the poet Dante as a
member of a formal religious order. Yet here he tells us quite
plainly that by means of the Franciscan cord he had intended
to "catch the leopard with the gaudy skin"—in other words,
to conquer the sins of youthful lust.[2] Does this mean that he
had at some point entered a monastery in hopes of atoning
for his past offenses against Beatrice and the purity of the
Romantic Vision?[3]

If so, it appears his plan was a failure. For in the episode
renarrated in this chapter (from *Inferno*, canto XVI), Dante
finds that the cord of religious discipline, instead of capturing
and taming the monster of *lussuria*, actually conjured up an
even more frightful beast: Geryon, the friendly faced, multicolored, venom-tailed serpent of the deep—the bright and
dazzling embodiment of Duplicity and Deceit.

In other words, *religion* failed Dante because it made
of him what it tends to make of all its devotees: a respect-
able fraud. And fraud, as it turns out, is the next logical step
in the poet's downwardly spiraling journey through Hell's
grim gallery of horrible might-have-beens. It's the next station on his nightmarish tour of the progressive perversion
of Romantic Love.

Here again there's a principle to be grasped. Once thrown
off-kilter and deflected from its original trajectory, self-
gratifying love does not simply take up residence in the circle

of the pleasure seekers. Unless something happens to arrest its decline, it sinks to even deeper levels of degradation. It begins with "you and me against the world." It slides imperceptibly into "you as an extension of my personal hedonism." In time it reaches the plane of systematic self-deception. Integrity dies, and the soul splits. A divided state of mind, aptly symbolized by Geryon, the three-headed, three-bodied monster of classical Greek mythology, lifts its head and rises from the pit.

The Bible has a word for this deplorable condition: *hypocrisy*. Jesus used it almost exclusively to describe extremely religious people—people like the scribes and Pharisees of first-century Judaism:

> Woe to you, scribes and Pharisees, hypocrites! For you cleanse the outside of the cup and dish, but inside they are full of extortion and self-indulgence. . . . You are like whitewashed tombs which indeed appear beautiful outwardly, but inside are full of dead men's bones and all uncleanness. (Matthew 23:25, 27)

Unclean cups. Whitewashed tombs. This is Christ's description of spiritual phoniness. But the illustration bears a broader application. In our present context it may also be seen as a disturbing image of what Dante's love for Beatrice *might* have become if allowed to swerve too far from the center of the circle. With the god of self in the ascendant, the belt of righteous-seeming summons up a hidden beast. Reality takes a backseat to appearance. Love itself becomes a formality, devoid of life and inward power. The face remains pleasant, but behind it swings a deadly scorpion's tail. In the upshot, the lover descends to Hell on the back of a smiling monster.

This is what Dante's mysterious reference to the cord

of the religious life is really all about. Religion, he says, is a poor substitute for Romance. Rituals, rules, and regulations are unmistakable marks of a love grown cold—stones on the grave of a dead passion.

"Israel has forgotten his Maker," moans Hosea, the prophet of Love, "and has built temples" (Hosea 8:14). The two activities often go hand in hand.

To put it another way, well-intentioned religious rigor, while it may begin with a legitimate desire to flee youthful lust, can become a cord that binds the soul. It can develop into a weed that chokes the romantic pathway of redemption by replacing the hope of a Redeemer with a boatload of impersonal obligations. When the risen Christ rebuked the Ephesian church, it was not for lack of religious zeal. It was because they had lost their first love (Revelation 2:4). Anyone who has known the earth-shattering, life-changing power of a first love—as Dante had known it on the streets of Florence—can appreciate the seriousness of the charge.

How do we hold on to that vision? How do we keep the flame of our first love alive? Dante has given us the answer. Like him, we must fling the belt of fraud and hypocrisy into the roiling abyss. We must be humble enough to stay honest, both in love and in the spiritual life: frank and free in our relationships with God and one another. And we must remain constantly on our guard against the temptation to believe in the goodness of our own self-centered schemes.

REFLECTION

Hypocrisy—whether of the Pharisee or the philanderer—is the constant enemy of Love.

FINAL DESTINATION

El fu si bello com'elli e ora brutto.

Once he was as fair as now he's foul.

—

Inferno, canto XXXIV, 34; trans. Mark Musa

FAR ACROSS THE ICE, vast and forbidding in the dim blue air, a dark blur loomed above the frozen surface of the lake. It reminded the pilgrim of something he had seen in his travels through the low countries: shadows of windmills on the foggy shoreline; tall, sail-armed ghosts laboring silently and grimly in the thick and clinging mist. But this was no windmill. It was far too big for that.

"'The banners of the king go forth,'" muttered Virgil, quoting the familiar Lenten hymn. "The banners of the king of *Hell*, that is." His forehead puckered as he pointed to the towering smudge on the horizon. "That, my friend, is none other than Dis. Hades. Lucifer. The devil himself—lord and most celebrated prisoner of this frigid dungeon. Look closely while you have the chance. It's not a sight you'll want to see again."

A chill crept into Dante's bones as his guide took him by

the elbow and drew him toward the dreadful apparition. As they came closer he could see that the gigantic figure stood chest high in the cracked and grating ice. Its body was covered with a thick, grimy pelt, and its six batlike wings beat the air unceasingly, fanning the perpetual winds that kept the waters of Lake Cocytus eternally frozen.

Most horrible of all was the monster's head. It bore three weeping and grimacing faces: yellow on the right, black on the left, scarlet in the middle. In each face was a slavering mouth, red like the maw of a beast of prey, and in each mouth a sinner writhed and twisted beneath the continual champing of the bloodstained teeth.

"The one on the left," said Virgil, "is Brutus. His counterpart on the right is Cassius. They assassinated their friend, ally, and leader, Julius Caesar. As for the one in the middle—the wretch who takes his punishment headfirst—that's Judas Iscariot."

Gazing up at the relentlessly working jaws, Dante could not help but be reminded of the unfortunate sufferers he'd already encountered—traitors and turncoats every one—during the course of his journey through these last and lowest circles of Hell. He thought of Count Ugolino, buried to the neck in ice and gnawing on the brain of his neighbor, Archbishop Ruggieri. He remembered how Ruggieri had merited such treatment: by betraying Ugolino and his four sons to imprisonment and death by starvation. He recalled the count's veiled hints of cannibalism during the final days of that unthinkable ordeal. Last of all, he pictured the ice-bound face of Fra Alberigo, the "jovial friar" who had invited his own brother to dinner and then called for his murder with the words "Bring on the fruit!" Gritting his teeth, he shuddered and turned away.

"Does this shock you?" asked Virgil, laying a hand on the pilgrim's shoulder. "It should. That creature was once the fairest of the sons of light. Now in the anguish of his own damnation, he grinds and chews the souls of his most faithful devotees."

"But how can such things be?"

"Here, at the center of the earth, we have reached the point farthest from the center of the Circle of *Amore*. This is the final destination of deflected love."

"Love?" cried Dante. "I see nothing here but hate! Obscene, violating, all-consuming hate!"

Virgil nodded. "Yes," he agreed. "Alarming, isn't it? I mean how easily—and, in some cases, how quickly—the one becomes the other."

In November 2004 a California jury convicted Scott Lee Peterson of murdering his wife, Laci, and their unborn child, Conner. The following March, Judge Alfred A. Delucchi sentenced Peterson to death by lethal injection, describing the defendant's crimes as "cruel, uncaring, heartless and callous."[1] Peterson himself has never ceased to maintain his innocence.

Innocent or guilty, Scott Peterson has become the central figure in a story that cannot fail to raise dark questions in the minds of all who ponder it. Perhaps the most dizzying and disturbing of all those questions is the one Dante faced as he stood gazing upon the monstrous form of Lucifer in the deepest pit of Hell: "How can such things be?"

How does a creature once beautiful become so foul and repulsive? How is the fairest of the sons of light transformed into the father of lies?

By the same token, how does love become hate? How could a man go from wooing, courting, and marrying a woman to killing her? At some point in Scott Peterson's experience, there must have been a day when he saw Laci Rocha approaching and said to himself—just as Dante had said of Beatrice—"Now your bliss draws near!" What could have driven him to destroy that bliss with his own two hands?

It would be easy to say that this tragic scenario is just a sign of the times in which we live, another example of postmodern amorality in action. Unfortunately, there is a great deal of evidence to suggest that Scott Peterson's story is as old as history itself; that it is, in fact, symptomatic of the human condition. In some ways, it echoes the Old Testament account of Amnon's passion for his half sister Tamar—a love that turned to contempt the moment Amnon had his way with her, "so that the hatred with which he hated her was greater than the love with which he had loved her" (2 Samuel 13:15). It's also oddly reminiscent of the many love/murder ballads that figure so prominently in popular folklore—traditional songs like "Little Omie Wise," for instance, which describes how John Lewis, after courting and impregnating Naomi Wise, led her down to the river where

> *He kissed her and hugged her and turned her around,*
> *Then pushed her in deep waters where he knew that*
> *   she would drown.*[2]

We may be sure that the first kiss John Lewis ever gave to Little Omie was a kiss of impassioned desire. The last was the kiss of death. That kiss is a perfect image of the sin we find punished in the deepest and blackest pit of Dante's Inferno: the sin of Judas Iscariot, the sin of *betrayal* and *treason*. Here, in the sinkhole at the base of Hell's funnel, is the place where "treachery gnaws treachery" in an ironic twist on its own two-timing inconstancy. Here, at the bottom of the world, is the frozen waste where faithlessness, by a process of self-compounding reduplication, is raised to the level of "infinite cannibalism."[3] It's a horrific prospect, particularly as Dante portrays it. But the most frightening thing about it is the realization that it all began with a profession of *love*.

How are such things possible? The answer may come as a shock. For the truth is that there is an exceedingly fine line between love and hate. From a certain perspective, they are like two sides of the same coin. It's even possible to argue that all hatred has its roots in misguided *Amore*.

That's because hate, like every other evil known to mankind, has no substance of its own. In itself it is nothing. It is only "a parasite on the good,"[4] a twisted parody of the virtue it mocks and maligns. This is why a college romance can end in a ghastly murder. This is how a man becomes capable of drowning the girl he once regarded as the desire of his heart. Love really is the most powerful force in the universe. And when it is deflected from its proper trajectory, it can, like an errant nuclear weapon, incur an incalculable amount of unintended damage.

To grasp this concept is to see the point of Dante's *Inferno*. Herein lies the lesson our poet is supposed to learn as he stands on the frozen surface of Lake Cocytus, contemplating the doom of the fallen angel of light. Dante could have ended up in a similar position had his love for Beatrice been allowed to stray too far from the center of the circle; and as we look back over the steps of his long infernal journey, we can easily imagine the stages by which this horrible transformation might have occurred:

It began with that moment of its suspended imagination in the Limbo, before, passing gently to its first consent, it yielded to the tender and poignant Francescan embrace; it descended a little farther to the indulgence of its own private appetites, no longer touched by a mutuality of love. . . . So, in the end, it becomes wholly false; it invokes treachery and cruelty; it has nothing to do but betray. . . . This is the end of the Way that began with the girl in Florence. . . . Dante has become Judas, and the power that champs him is what was once Beatrice.[5]

Scripture expresses it this way: "There is a way that seems right to a man, but its end is the way of death" (Proverbs 14:12).

As of this writing, Scott Peterson remains on San Quentin's death row, awaiting the appeal of his case to the California Supreme Court. His story, like Dante's, began with the flame of *Amore*. Unlike the Florentine poet's, it has ended in disaster. How can such things be?

We know the answer. We have seen how off-centered love moves from *lussuria* and self-indulgence to fraud, deception, and death. We have watched the romantic dream morph into a horrific nightmare. We have seen how the Vision is twisted and destroyed. What we desperately need now is to learn how this lethal trajectory can be reversed.

And that's precisely what Dante intends to show us next— in his narrative of the trek up the sides of Mount Purgatory.

REFLECTION

Hate is simply Love distorted beyond all recognition.

GETTING PERSONAL
When Love Goes Astray

THROUGHOUT THE INFERNO, Dante encounters men and women reaping the consequence of considering love only as it benefits themselves—the first misstep toward a gravelly descent. Their filthy scabs, skin-scraped limbs, and bloodied hands remind us just how treacherous the downward momentum of selfishness can become.

One doesn't need to look far to realize one of God's great treasures has been tarnished—twisted into an unsightly mockery of its original design. Men use women as faceless objects to satisfy carnal urges—creating callous souls lingering around the scorching flames of pornography, prostitution, and perversion. Meanwhile, women join Tina Turner singing, "What's love got to do with it?" while seducing men as toys to manipulate or trophies to win. Each alluring look, lustful gaze, and illicit encounter reduces those made in the image of God into caricatures of wallowing swine.

Even those who avoid the dishonor of sexual sin can find themselves slipping and sliding down a slope of broken relationships. Pouting and fighting replace thoughtful gestures. Cantankerous tantrums drown out patient warmth. Selfish demands overtake selfless devotion.

Ugly sights to behold. Even uglier to become.

In order to avoid your own slide downward, ask yourself a few questions that will personalize lessons learned during Dante's trip to the slope's tragic bottom.

QUESTION 1: ARE YOU MOVING UPHILL OR DOWNHILL?

Love reaps life; lust steals it away. And as Dante discovered, the virus of lust goes much deeper than the impure thought or illicit affair. These are mere symptoms of a much greater problem.

Trace every marital spat, sexual indiscretion, divorce proceeding, or adulterous affair to its first misstep, and you will find the same basic blunder. One or both parties traded Christ's call to selfless giving for the indulgence of selfish grasping. In other words, they replaced love with lust. Rather than putting others before themselves, they saw others as useful *for* themselves. Or in the case of broken relationships, no longer useful enough.

The real tragedy, of course, is the loss of potential. The promise of joy squandered, budding life killed, an aspiring romantic masterpiece marred into something more suited for the Dumpster than a gallery wall.

"There is but one good; that is God. Everything else is good when it looks to Him and bad when it turns from Him," wrote C. S. Lewis of our descent. "And the higher and mightier it is in the natural order, the more demoniac it will be if it rebels. It's not out of bad mice or bad fleas you make demons, but out of bad archangels."[1] Precisely because we are God's highest creation, lust turns men and women into something worse than demons.

Self-centered living always lands us at the stony bottom surrounded by the broken bodies of those we took down with us—possibly a betrayed spouse, a diseased lover, an estranged family, or an abandoned child. Looking around in regret, we realize too late that Solomon was right. "There *is* a way that seems right" but that leads to death (Proverbs 16:25).

Death of relationships.

Death of beauty.

Death of our own dignity.

And what do we get in exchange? A shoddy counterfeit of what we might have had and what we might have become.

"Lust is a poor, weak, whimpering, whispering thing compared with that richness and energy of desire which will arise when lust has been killed,"[2] said Lewis about mankind's voluntary descent into hell. What triggers the descent? What he calls defective love—perverting its intended momentum by placing ourselves at the center of a galaxy called "me, myself, and I." And when that which was created to *give* begins instead to *take*, it becomes deformed.

So be honest with yourself. What missteps can you repent to get yourself back on the upward path? Have you hurt your beloved through selfish demands? Have you been unfaithful in thought or deed? Have you diminished yourself or disrespected another?

It is never too late to turn around and begin climbing back. Doing so, however, will certainly require the help and guidance of one much wiser than yourself.

QUESTION 2: DO YOU LISTEN TO THE WISDOM OF THOSE WHO HAVE BEEN WHERE YOU HOPE TO GO?

As he begins his romantic journey, Dante meets his literary hero, an ancient poet named Virgil. He is a perfect guide since Virgil's writings served as a model and mentor for Dante's own. Throughout *The Divine Comedy*, Virgil gently leads Dante through Love's treacherous valleys and boosts him up its steep embankments. You see, Virgil knew the best paths. He had already been where Dante was going.

We all need the direction of older, wiser mentors—especially in matters of the heart. Unfortunately, advice is the last thing many of us want when we're romantically involved. Encouragement, yes. Well wishes and registry gifts, you bet. But when it comes to the who, whether, and how of love, we prefer following our giddy hearts to seeking wise counsel.

It's an odd thing. We often can't select a restaurant entrée without asking the opinion of others. But when making the most impactful decisions in life, we fly solo. If a total stranger recommends a side dish, we thank and tip him or her. But when people who love us suggest we slow down a relationship that appears harmful, we tell them to mind their own business.

How dumb is that? According to the Scriptures, very dumb indeed.

- "He who trusts in his own heart is a fool." (Proverbs 28:26)
- "The way of a fool is right in his own eyes, but he who heeds counsel is wise." (Proverbs 12:15)
- "A fool despises his father's instruction, but he who receives correction is prudent." (Proverbs 15:5)
- "In a multitude of counselors there is safety." (Proverbs 24:6)

Once upon a time, it was normal for those navigating the ups and downs of romantic love to seek advice from parents, siblings, trusted friends, and godly mentors. The couple's union was nurtured in the rich soil of community, so more of Love's seeds grew into strong, stable trees.

How times have changed! Couples are now left to fend for themselves. Children not even old enough to drive a car are invited into the volatile world of romantic love. Even parents, the ones who historically chose a child's mate, have withdrawn from the coaching process. The Christian community, which should be a flourishing garden of shared wisdom and support, operates more like a collection of independent flowerpots.

When was the last time you asked those who know you best whether your dating relationship is characterized by respect and restraint? Does anyone challenge you to make your marriage a picture of self-sacrifice and humility, grace and forgiveness?

Dante avoided fatal missteps in his pursuit of lasting, intimate joy by heeding the older, wiser Virgil. He understood the value of wise counsel and of listening to someone who had been where he hoped to go.

When it comes to your love life, can the same be said of you?

Like watching a snow-laced boulder grow as it races down the mountain, we have seen with Dante the degrading results of defective love. We have heard him speak to those who let the momentum of their downward descent overtake any will to resist. So armed with the knowledge of what he must avoid, Dante now seeks to learn how we can redirect the love kindled in innocence toward its intended object and end—our beautiful God of redemption.

PART 3

Love Fulfilled

Purgatory and Paradise

*Perchè la faccia mia sì t'innamora
che tu non ti rivolgi al bel giardino
che sotto i raggi di Cristo s'infiora?*

Why are you so enamored of my face
that you do not turn to the lovely garden
flowering in the radiance of Christ?

—

PARADISE, CANTO XXIII, 70–72; TRANS. MARK MUSA

PRESS ON!

Qual negligenza, quale stare è questo?
Correte al monte a spogliarvi lo scoglio.

Why all this dawdling? why this negligence?
Run to the mountains, slough away the filth.

—

Purgatory, canto II, 121–122; trans. Dorothy Sayers

THE SKY! HE THOUGHT as he stood on the sand, gazing out across the darkly gleaming waves. Bands of light, vermilion and rose, lay glowing on the horizon. Above them the stars of morning sparkled like diamonds in a setting of sapphire. Dante shrugged, as if shedding a heavy burden. *I had almost forgotten . . .*

Already the details of their unimaginable tour of the infernal regions were slipping into the realm of dim remembrance: the horrible three-headed fiend; the impossible climb up his woolly flanks; the tight squeeze through the earth's core; their emergence into the fragrant dawn of a southern isle. Had it all really happened?

"And how does *he*, a living man, come within the boundaries of my realm?"

Dante and Virgil turned at the sound of a stern voice. Before them stood a venerable old man in a long, white robe. He scanned them with his steel-blue eyes.

"My lord Cato," Virgil said, bowing low, "honored guardian of Purgatory. This man is here at the request of a heavenly lady. She awaits him on the mountaintop."

Cato grunted. "In that case, clean the Hell-grime from his face with the morning dew. Gird him with a reed from the shore. Then move on. Quickly. The sun will show you the way up the mountainside." With that, he spun on his heel and left them.

So Dante was cleansed and girded. And as he lifted his head from the washing, he saw a sudden light out on the ocean. Brighter and closer it grew with every passing moment. So rapid was its approach that they could soon see quite clearly what it was: a great, white ship, driven by the wings of an angelic steersman, filled with souls singing the ancient psalm: "When Israel went out of Egypt . . ."

"Dante! Dante Alighieri!" cried one of the travelers as the ship touched the shore and its passengers flung themselves upon the sand. "To think I'd find you *here*!"

"Casella!" Dante shouted in answer. "The bard of Pistoia! The sweetest voice in all of Tuscany! Give us a song, old friend?"

"I'll go you one better," Casella said, laughing. "I'll give you one of your own!" And with that he threw back his head and began to sing: *"Amor che ne la mente mi ragiona."*

Except for his voice all was still on that peaceful, radiant shore. Every soul fell silent under the enchantment of the music. It was Easter morning. A pale, transparent blue was creeping up the slope of the cloudless sky. Dante felt as if time had stopped. Casting a glance at his companion, he saw a smile stirring the corners of Virgil's lips.

"And just *what* do you think you're all doing?"

Again that voice! Again the sharp rebuke! Instantly the spell was broken. Every head whipped round as the dying notes of Casella's half-sung song dissolved in the air. Cato stood above them on a rocky knoll.

"This is no time for merrymaking!" he said, shaking his finger and scowling like a thundercloud. "Have you forgotten why you're here? Don't you know there's a mountain to climb?"

An instant later the entire crowd was scrambling up the lower slopes like a flock of birds before an approaching storm.

Perhaps you know what it's like to have been through hell and come out on the other side. If so, you'll understand what was going through Dante's mind as he stepped out of the fetid blackness of the Inferno and into the fragrant air of the mountain island of Purgatory.

After a dizzying two-day trek down the spiraling galleries of the damned, through the squeeze-hole at the center of the earth, and up the sunless tunnels beyond, most of us would be ready for a vacation. Most of us would feel that we had earned a few days' relaxation and rest. Dante must have been imagining naps in the sand and leisurely strolls in the afternoon sun as he stood on Purgatory's shore, kissed by the pre-dawn breeze of a morning in spring. But it wasn't to be.

Ecclesiastes tells us that there is a time for everything: a time to plant and a time to reap; a time to laugh and a time to weep; a time for mourning and a time for dancing; a time to win and a time to lose (Ecclesiastes 3:1-8). Even common wisdom suggests that play follows work and labor is rewarded with rest. But when we tread the pathway of romance, a different set of rules applies. The time to dedicate ourselves to the work of love—diligently and with thoughtful care—is always *now*.

That's the lesson Dante learns in the opening scene of

Purgatory, the second canticle of *The Divine Comedy*. He and Virgil and a crowd of penitent souls stand spellbound on the windswept beach, lost in a moment of pleasure and leisure, transfixed by the beauty of Casella's ethereal song. Abruptly Cato, the island's implacable guardian, steps in with a stirring cry. "Get moving!" he shouts. "There may be a place for pleasantries, *but this isn't it!* You people are here because you have work to do!"

In an important sense, these words epitomize the whole purpose of Dante's Purgatory. It's here that the distortions and errors of the Inferno begin to be undone. It's here that the Romantic Vision is reclaimed and set firmly on the road to redemption. Here we are invited to ask, "What if the true Way of *Amore* had in fact been followed? What if imagination, rather than wandering from the center of the circle, had willed to become faith instead?"[1] The answer, of course, is that it would have become a stairway to the stars.

No wonder Cato urges Dante and his fellow travelers to make haste. *Love* is waiting at the top of the steep-sided mountain. Beatrice herself beckons from its peak. With such a goal in view, why linger in the lowlands? Why not begin *now* to overcome the barriers that bar the way to fulfillment?

This theme of urgency surfaces again and again during the course of Dante's ascent of Mount Purgatory—most poignantly, perhaps, in the words of the souls he encounters on the Terrace of Sloth:

> *Faster! faster, we have no time to waste,*
> *for time is love.*[2]

Time is love. That's why time is truly of the essence. That's why lovers need to begin "redeeming the time" (Ephesians

5:16; Colossians 4:5). They dare not allow the sun to go down on the roots of alienation or anger (Ephesians 4:26). When the Vision has gone astray, *Amore* demands that all be done—and done *now*—to restore it to its original trajectory.

Ironically, this is exactly the point of the "amorous song" (*cantico amoroso*) that Casella, Dante's musician friend, sings on the shores of the island. It's a lyric of Dante's own composition: "Love that reasons with me in my mind."[3] Our author has a good reason for introducing it here. In *La Vita Nuova*, Dante appealed for help to those ladies of Florence who possessed "intelligence in love."[4] Elsewhere in the same book, he boldly referred to Beatrice herself as *nobile intelletto*, "noble intelligence." At the gate of the Inferno he learned that Hell is the abode of that "suffering race of souls who lost the good of intellect."[5] Casella's song takes up the same refrain. It reminds our hero once again that it is only a *reasonable love*—a love that engages the mind as well as the heart, the passions, and the lower instincts—that leads to the longed-for reunion at the top of the mountain.

Why a "*reasonable*" love? Because only such a love is capable of grasping the urgency of the situation. Only an intelligent love sees the need to apply thought and foresight to the practical outworking of passion, to reorder perspectives and priorities so as to keep the beloved at the center of the circle. As Charles Williams observes,

> Dante insists on the "in my mind," for it is there that this affection for truth and virtue exists. The aspect of the beloved "aids our faith," just as it "renovates nature." But the mind has to work on it, and so has faith, and it is this which, it seems, Paolo and Francesca have not done.[6]

Paul's love for Christ, like Dante's love for Beatrice, was a love that "reasoned with him in his mind." It entailed a complete renovation of the intellect (Romans 12:2). *Passion* inspired him to aim for the peak of the mountain. *Intelligence* told him what he had to do in order to reach it:

> But what things were gain to me, these I have counted loss for Christ. Yet indeed I also count all things loss for the excellence of the knowledge of Christ Jesus my Lord, for whom I have suffered the loss of all things, and count them as rubbish, that I may gain Christ. . . . Not that I have already attained, or am already perfected; but I press on, that I may lay hold of that for which Christ Jesus has also laid hold of me. (Philippians 3:7-8, 12)

Press on! This is the substance of Cato's exhortation to the souls he finds dawdling at the base of Mount Purgatory. It is an exhortation meant for every lover in every circumstance of life. For if the Romantic Vision is worth serving at all, it is worth serving with diligence, intelligence, and intentionality. After all, Lady Love doesn't like to be kept waiting.

REFLECTION

First things first.

THE SEED

Quinci comprender puoi ch'esser convene
amor sementa in voi d'ogne virtute
e d'ogne operazion che merta pene.

Thus you may understand that love alone
is the true seed of every merit in you,
and of all acts for which you must atone.

—

Purgatory, canto XVII, 103–105; trans. John Ciardi

"I'M SORRY, MASTER," gasped the pilgrim, collapsing on the topmost stair, "but it seems my strength and breath have run out!"

The last rays of sunlight had faded from the rocks, and one by one the stars were beginning to blink overhead. Far below, the sea was merging with the mist along the dim ribbon of shoreline. Virgil smiled and sat down beside him. "It's the law of the mountain," he said. "No climbing after dark."

Dante touched his forehead. Already three of the seven *P*s had been smoothed away. The Terraces of Pride, Envy, and Wrath lay behind them. They were halfway up the mountain. He sighed and wiped the sweat from his brow.

"What terrace is this?" he asked, squinting into the gathering gloom. "What offense is purged here?"

Suddenly, from around the bend of the cornice, there came

the thunder of running feet. A crowd of naked souls pounded past, sprinting at top speed and shouting slogans as they zipped by: "Time is Love! No time to waste! Hurry! Hurry! Hurry!"

"There's your answer!" the old Roman said, laughing in response to his companion's bewildered stare. "These people are learning to pursue Love with all their strength. For Love is the Spring and the Source. It's the fundamental fact. And this is the Terrace of the Negligent in Love: the Slothful, the Lazy, the Lackadaisical."

"What do you mean, 'the fundamental fact'?"

Virgil leaned back against the rock and closed his eyes. "Isn't it obvious?" he said. "Love is the reason for everything you do. It's like the upward leaping of the flame. You see something. You want it. You go after it. It's the story of your life."

"But that's not *Love*," Dante objected. "What you're describing is an *attraction*. An *impulse*. And not all impulses are good. We've seen enough to know *that*!"

"Yes. But good or bad, these impulses, as you call them, are still a part of the soul's quest: an expression of longing, an admission of need. I will readily grant that they lead different people in different directions. Take the Proud, the Envious, and the Wrathful—*they* tried to meet their need by eliminating all competition. And the folks on the terraces above—the Greedy, the Gluttonous, and the Lustful—went after *good* things in a *bad* way. As for the runners you just saw, they simply didn't care enough to get involved. They're just now joining the race. Better late than never."

A long silence followed. At last Dante said, "But if what you're saying about the 'quest' of the soul is true, then these people aren't to blame. It's not *their* fault if they were attracted to something and pursued it. You don't condemn the flame for leaping. And you can't control your 'natural inclinations.'"

Virgil raised his head and opened his eyes. "Ah!" he said. "But you can! You can because you *know*. You understand the difference between *right* and *wrong*!"

Dante frowned. "Am I really free to make that choice?" he asked.

Virgil gave him a wink. "That, my friend," he said, "is a question for Beatrice."

Halfway through the second canticle of *The Divine Comedy*, at the mathematical midpoint of Dante's pilgrimage, Virgil pauses at the gateway to Mount Purgatory's middle terrace, the Terrace of Sloth, to deliver a lecture on the nature and meaning of Love.

What does the old Roman tell his pupil at this strategic juncture in the story? Simply that *Amore*—that imperious "god" whom Dante has been serving since the early chapters of *La Vita Nuova*—is absolutely central to *everything*. It's the fountainhead to which all of our actions, both good *and* evil, can ultimately be traced.

This isn't a new idea. Those who have followed Dante this far have already seen it illustrated in a number of different ways. But not until now has the pilgrim's guide had the leisure to explain its connection to the poem's central theme: mankind's upward journey to the stars.

Why is Love such a vital part of that journey? Primarily because human beings are designed to function as *seekers*. Men and women, as creatures made in God's image, are meant to live their lives in search of a true and genuine Other: something or Someone to complete the dimly perceived *partialness* of their existence.

All of you, vaguely, apprehend and crave
a good with which your heart may be at rest;
and so, each of you strives to reach that goal.[1]

There is, of course, only one "Good in which the heart may rest": God Himself.[2] Ultimately, *He* is the One we are trying to find in all of our seeking and blind groping (Acts 17:27). But hearts dulled by sin don't realize this. Slumbering in a shroud of self-imposed darkness and death, they have no clear conception of their own wants and needs. That's where *Amore* comes in.

Love is the power that wakes the heart and lures it from the tomb. Love entices men and women to pursue the quest. By means of some "vague apprehension" of the Good, it puts its hooks into us and drags us into the light. It provides us with a tangible and comprehensible *image* of the desired *Other*. It gives shape and definition to our longings.

Here's how it works. An object external to myself—a dazzlingly beautiful woman like Beatrice, for instance—attracts my attention. It stamps its firm imprint into the soft wax of my perceptions. This impression becomes for me a personalized icon of the fulfillment and joy I seek. Everything within me inclines toward it. I feel I cannot rest until I have laid hold of it. As a result, I burst from my self-centered cocoon in a focused effort to achieve it. *This*, according to Dante's mentor, is the anatomy of *Amore*. *This* is the seed from which the tree of human life and action sprouts and grows.

But Virgil hastens to add a warning. The seed of Love does not always grow aright. Unless properly watered and nurtured, it cannot, like Jack's beanstalk, become a stairway to the sky, for it carries within itself a dual potentiality. Under the right conditions, as in the case of the young Dante, it may produce the fruit of the Romantic Vision, leading us to understand that God alone fulfills the desires of our hearts (Psalm 37:4). But if neglected or abused, as in the story of Paolo and Francesca, it can morph into a noxious weed of indulgence and deceit, creating a situation in which our desires for pleasure incite us to lust, fight, covet, and murder, though we still end up empty-handed (James 4:1-3).

The need for Dante's Purgatory arises directly out of this dual potentiality. For Purgatory is above all a place where redemption is accomplished by means of the rehabilitation of Loves.[3] It's in Purgatory that the Proud, the Envious, and the Wrathful are taught to prize their neighbor above their personal "apprehensions" of the Good. It's in Purgatory that the Greedy, the Gluttonous, and the Lustful learn to reprioritize their natural attachments to God's good gifts. And it's in Purgatory that the Slothful—those who have lost interest in the quest—find the means to rekindle the fire in their souls.

To put it another way, Dante's Purgatory exists because Loves can be either good or bad. But this leads to another question. If *Amore* originates as an involuntary response to an outward stimulus, as Virgil claims, where does the question of right and wrong come in? Why blame a poor sinner for following the impulses of human nature and answering the call of an irresistible image? That's what Dante wants to know at this crucial point in the dialogue.

> *If love comes from a source outside of us,*
> *the soul having no choice, how can you praise*
> *or blame it for its love of good or bad?*[4]

Here again Virgil's response has a familiar ring. For he tells his pupil that a *good* Love is a reasonable Love. It's the

87

Love of those Florentine ladies who possessed intelletto d'Amore.[5] It's the Love that "speaks to me within my mind."[6] This Love entails thought, moral discernment, and a disciplined imagination. It requires and desires "the strength which counsels and ought to control assent":

> It is at this point that the question of good or bad enters. For all things must be loved in order and after their proper kind and with (as one may say) the proper form—the manner and ceremony that belongs to it.[7]

In other words, we *can* love rightly because we have been granted the ability to think and choose. We are not mere victims of passion but rational agents in a world of clear moral imperatives, knowing the difference between dark and light; vice and virtue; good, better, and best. We need not, like Francesca and Paolo, fall prey to the winds of *lussuria*.

This, Virgil adds significantly, is what Beatrice calls *Freedom of the Will*.[8] And Beatrice ought to know. For unlike the pagan poet Virgil, Beatrice, a Christian, knows the ins and outs of the soul's continuing struggle against sin. She realizes that Dante may object: "I'm not as free as you suppose. Many times I have tried and failed to choose what's right. 'The good that I will to do, I do not do; but the evil I will not to do, that I practice. . . . O wretched man that I am! Who will deliver me from this body of death?'" (Romans 7:19, 24).

The answer, of course, lies beyond the peak of Mount Purgatory. It is hidden, as Virgil plainly states, with Beatrice herself. For in the final analysis, Beatrice is only Dante's "vague apprehension" of a much greater reality—the reality of God's amazing grace. She is his personal *image* of the final

Truth, the ultimate Good in which alone the heart can rest.
And it's in this role that she must guide him at last to the
highest heights of the blessed realm.

REFLECTION

*The seed of Love flourishes in the
soil of grace and good sense.*

A RUDE WELCOME

Guardaci ben! Ben son, ben son Beatrice.
Come degnasti d'accedere al monte?

Look at me well. I am she. I am Beatrice.
How dared you make your way to this high mountain?

—

Purgatory, canto XXX, 73–74; trans. John Ciardi

A SUDDEN TREMOR in the treetops. A blaze of light and a cry
of "*Hosanna!*" A breath of air and a thunderclap. And then—
silence like the stillness of deep heaven itself.

Dante stood trembling at the edge of the stream, gaping
in wonder as the procession drew up on the far bank. Never
in his life could he have imagined such a dazzling display.
Seven golden candlesticks trailing pennants of rainbow flame.
Twenty-four elders, robed in white and crowned with lilies.
Four celestial creatures, covered with wings and eyes. Seven
dancing ladies and seven rose-wreathed sages. In their midst
padded a great gryphon, half golden eagle and half ruddy
lion. And in the gryphon-drawn chariot rode a lady—a lady
with burning emerald eyes.

He knew her at once in spite of her unaccustomed attire:
the scarlet robe, the green cloak, the garland of olive branches,
the white veil across her face. He saw her plainly in spite of

the curtain of lilies that fell around her in a translucent cascade. When her eyes locked with his, his heart leapt into his throat. He felt he would burst with mingled terror and joy.

"The old flame!" he whispered, the blood rushing to his head. "I know it, Virgil! I know it well!" He wheeled around to catch his guide by the sleeve. But Virgil was nowhere to be seen.

The words caught in his throat. A sense of sudden realization swept over him. *Gone.* His beloved guide was gone. He stumbled. He hesitated. Hot, stinging tears started into his eyes. And then a voice like liquid gold flowed down over him from above.

"*Dante.*" The hair rose on the back of his neck. She was calling him by name! "Dante, do not weep," she said; then added, "at least *not yet.*"

Not yet. The words lodged in his brain like a couple of small, sharp stones. What could they mean? Wasn't this the top of the mountain? Hadn't he left all cause for weeping behind? Wasn't the long-awaited reunion at hand?

Slowly he turned and looked up to where she stood gazing down upon him from behind the gryphon's golden head. Her eyes blazed—those same green eyes that had captured his heart in Florence and sustained him throughout the whole of his unthinkable journey. She towered over him like a mythical queen, like an Amazon maiden in a shining chariot of war. He made a feeble attempt to smile.

"Yes!" she said at last—but her eyes did not smile—"I *am* Beatrice! You were perhaps expecting someone else?"

He squirmed. His face fell. "N-no," he began.

"How is it," she interrupted, "that you had the nerve to come here?"

"I—" he faltered. "I mean *you* . . . I mean *Virgil* said that you . . ."

"Look at me!" she said. "Hold your beard up, little man! Prepare to give an account of yourself. You have a lot of explaining to do."

At that his tears began to flow in streams.

Love, as Virgil has told us, is a *quest*. And it is the nature of every quest to run straight on toward its goal. It *must* succeed. It *cannot* fail. There is no other option.

How ironic, then, that so many questing stories end in ambiguity. How remarkable that so few can be described simply as successful or unsuccessful in terms of the hero's initial intentions. Columbus set a course for the Indies and wound up in the Bahamas. Dorothy Gale dreamed of blue skies over the rainbow but discovered "there's no place like home." The road to fulfillment is filled with strange surprises.

Sometimes, as in the examples just cited, the end of that road is as happy as it is unanticipated. But in other instances it's more like a slap in the face. Consider the plight of Bilbo Baggins and friends, who claimed a treasure but roused a dragon in the process. Or Ulysses, who pursued immortality but got death and damnation instead (see *Inferno* XXVI). King Arthur's knights sought the Holy Grail but found only evidence of their own unworthiness for the task.[1] Many quests come to a rudely twisted end.

That's how it happened with Dante. *The Divine Comedy* is the story of his quest for reunion with his beloved Beatrice. It was the hope of seeing her again that led him through the dark and icy depths of Hell. It was the thought of her eyes that steeled him to scale Mount Purgatory's craggy cliffs and brave the wall of fire on the Terrace of Lust. At the end of his trek, it was her appearance in glory that reawakened the

Romantic Vision in his soul. Surely he was right to expect bliss and nothing but bliss from that point forward!

What a shock, then, when what he received instead was a withering rebuke. "Yes, I am Beatrice!" he heard the lady say. "Take a good look and see me for what I *am*! As you look, learn well what I am not! For I am not a mere projection of yourself. I am not just the embodiment of your dreams. I am in fact myself. And as such, I have certain expectations of you."

A rude welcome indeed for the weary traveler—as shocking to the reader as to the pilgrim himself. After all, wasn't it Beatrice who summoned Dante in the first place? Isn't she the most important link in the Chain of Love that rescued him from the depths of Hell? Why, then, does she question his motives in coming?

The answer takes us straight to the center of Love's circle. For it is in this moment of truth that Dante, like the heroes of so many quests gone awry, learns what it means to *grow up*. Under the blaze of his lady's eyes he realizes that the Romantic Vision often leads to an unanticipated end. As her harsh words are spoken, his dream fades and his quest appears to fall flat. But he gains an unexpected prize in the process—the prize of Maturity in Love.

Maturity in Love. This is the point of Dante's shocking reception at the top of Mount Purgatory. All who are experienced in the ways of *Amore* will recognize it. They will resonate, however painfully, with Beatrice's reminder that the beloved deserves to be regarded as *a person in his or her own right*—a true and genuine other. They will understand that there is an important sense in which a marriage cannot begin until the honeymoon is over. They will know that there can be no relationship, no consummation, no *in-othering* of themselves in the sweet, solid reality of someone else until they are willing to face hard facts and *do* something about them.

It's significant that this breakthrough comes precisely at the moment of Virgil's disappearance. Now that Dante stands face-to-face with Beatrice, his personal image of the highest Good, the old Roman's task as mentor is complete. It is time now for the pilgrim to lift his chin and start behaving like a man (1 Corinthians 16:13, KJV). The irony, of course, is that he can do this only by becoming like a child (Mark 10:15)— by finding the courage to acknowledge his faults with earnest groans and tears (Psalm 6:6).

"How did you *dare* to climb this mountain?" Beatrice demands as those tears well up in his eyes. Her question is pregnant with meaning. As Charles Williams points out, the Italian *come degnasti* might be better translated as "how did you *deign* or *condescend* to climb?"[2] In other words, the pilgrim has reached this all-important stage in the journey for one reason only: he has been willing to *humble* himself. This is what it means to *grow up* in the ways of Love. "Dante has had to be moved and persuaded and commanded and threatened before he would condescend to be happy; he has almost had to be scared into joy," says Williams.[3]

Humility. Maturity. Joy. They go together like root and stem and fruit. *That's* what Jesus means when He says that a grain of wheat cannot produce a crop unless it first falls into the ground and dies (John 12:24). *That's* what He has in mind when He declares that the way to find your life is to lose it (Matthew 10:39). Every human heart is engaged in a quest. But in the economy of Christ's Kingdom, that quest is fulfilled only when it has come to a shockingly twisted end.

The connection between this teaching of Jesus and Dante's poetic theme is no coincidence. For Christ Himself is present at the reunion on the mountaintop. He dominates the scene in the shape of the mythical gryphon, whose dual form, combining features of both eagle and lion, is a poetic image of the two-natured Son of God. He reveals Himself in the eyes of Beatrice, wherein Dante clearly perceives the "twy-formed" beast, and thus the God-man Himself, reflected as in two shining mirrors:

> *Like sunlight in a glass the twofold creature*
> *shone from the deep reflection of her eyes,*
> *now in the one, now in the other nature.*[4]

Here, for the first time, Dante tells us plainly what he has been suggesting all along: that the quest for Romantic Love, if kept pure and true, must eventually become a quest for the Savior. Here he declares openly what he has been hinting ever since the earliest chapters of *La Vita Nuova*: that God Himself is the unexpected object of *Amore*'s deepest longings.

This may be the most shocking thing about the twist that awaits us at the conclusion of Dante's pilgrimage up the mountainside. But it is by no means the end of the story. For as we are soon to discover, the best is yet to come.

REFLECTION

Humility is the key to Maturity in Love.

CONTENTMENT

I' son Piccarda
Che, posta qui con questi altri beati,
Beata sono in la spera più tarda.

[I am]
Piccarda, that with all this blessèd host
Joined in the slowest sphere, am blessèd too.
—

Paradise, canto III, 49–51; trans. Dorothy Sayers

THUS IT CAME ABOUT that Dante, his memories purged, his mind renewed, his soul washed clean in the flow of his own tears, stood poised at last on the peak of Mount Purgatory with nothing but the bright air between him and the rolling spheres of the nine heavens. His gaze was fixed immovably upon his lady's face. But she, head thrown back and green eyes wide, was staring directly into the flaming heart of the sun.

Without thinking, the pilgrim followed her lead. To his great surprise, he discovered that after the first few seconds of searing blindness his vision grew so clear and strong that he could actually *see*, not merely the glory of the solar corona, but the burning inner essence of the sun itself. In the next instant, he and Beatrice were rocketing skyward like two bolts of inverted lightning.

"Look out!" he cried; for he could see that they were headed straight for what appeared to be a large, solid sphere of pearly luminescence. But before the words were out of his mouth the roar of their flight fell to sudden silence and he found himself *inside* the shining globe, suspended in the milky, richly marbled stuff of its interior.

"How is it possible," he stammered, "that one body—mine—should be taken up into another—this celestial pearl—without so much as a clash or a crash?"

Beatrice beamed. Her eyes shone like the sun itself. "Such is the law of this place," she said. "It is only the beginning of wonders."

Peering about him, he saw what looked like faces swimming before his eyes, dim and translucent like reflections on a windowpane. Glancing over his shoulder, he scanned his surroundings to find the source of these mirrored images. No one was there.

Beatrice laughed. "These are not mere likenesses," she said, "but actual substances. Blessed souls of real people. Look! One of them wants to speak with you!"

He turned. A faintly radiant shape was moving toward him: a pale but beautiful woman.

"Don't you know me, Dante?" she asked. "I am Piccarda! Sister of your friend Forese Donati! On earth I took the veil and sought to live as Christ's bride. But my other brother—the cruel Corso—snatched me from the cloister and forced me to marry one of his political allies. I am here, in the lowest and slowest of all heaven's spheres, because I was compelled to break my vow." Her eyes danced with delight.

"Lowest and slowest?" The pilgrim stared. "Then why so happy? Have you no longing to move up higher? Nearer to the center? Closer to God?"

Her silvery laughter took him off guard. "What an idea!" she exclaimed. "His will *is* the center! His will is our peace! And for me, His will is *here*. This, too, is heaven. Think carefully about what Love really is, and I believe you'll see what I mean."

With that, like a pearl in dark water, she faded from his view, lightly singing a hymn of praise; and Dante, as if drawn by an irresistible attraction, turned again to his lady.

So dazzling had her beauty become that he was almost forced to cover his eyes.

In our journeys with Dante we have discovered that Love is a *quest*. Lovers, as Virgil has explained, are seekers. And *Amore* is the force that stirs them up, shakes them out, and compels them to go in search of their heart's desire.

That quest invariably begins in a golden haze of sweetness and light. The pathway, too, is frequently marked by excitement and thrills. But what becomes of the Romantic Vision when the Mountain has been scaled, the longed-for reunion has been realized, and the envisioned Paradise lies within the pilgrim's grasp at last? Does Love continue after the adventure reaches its climax? This is one of the questions Dante tackles in the third and final canticle of his *Divina Commedia*, the *Paradiso*.

In *On Monarchy* (*De Monarchia*), a political treatise written several years prior to the *Comedy*, Dante says that God has designed everybody and everything to *fit* a particular slot somewhere. Each one of us is meant to thrive *in operatione propriae virtutis*—that is, in the exercise of his or her proper function.[1] "A place for everything and everything in its place"—this, according to our poet, is the controlling principle of a harmonious human society. In the *Paradiso*, it also becomes the basis for the ordering of the heavenly spheres.

Contrary to modern popular opinion, the medievals did *not* believe in a flat earth. Their world and their universe were both decidedly round. They conceived of the heavens as a hierarchy of concentric circles: a series of vast transparent globes, one revolving within another, at the center of which hung the earth like a tiny blue marble in the midst of a great hollow ball. Beyond the ninth sphere, that of the Fixed Stars, lay the eternal Empyrean, the abode of God Himself. Immediately above the earth rolled the dimly glowing orb of the ever-changing Moon.[2] It's here, in the sphere of the Moon, the lowest and slowest-moving of all the nine heavenly circles, that Dante encounters Piccarda Donati, kinswoman of his wife, Gemma, and sister of his longtime friend Forese.[3] It's here, Piccarda assures him, that she has *found her place* in the divine plan.

The reason for her assignment to this relatively humble station—this heaven of the saved but faint and inconstant souls—is simple: she made a vow to God and broke it. True, she was *forced* to break it against her will. But the fact remains that her devotion was imperfect. Dante will spend the greater part of the next two cantos wrestling with the deeper implications of Piccarda's fate. But for the time being, what surprises and impresses him most about this meek but shining soul is her attitude: she actually seems to be *happy* in her situation.

How can this be, he wonders? If Paradise is a matter of reaching and touching the highest and greatest Good, why stop *here*, on the bottom step of the upward climbing stair? If that Good resides in God alone, as Beatrice has indicated, shouldn't Piccarda be hoping to move a few rungs farther up the ladder? Isn't she eager to join the contemplatives in the sphere of Saturn? the just rulers of Jupiter? the champions of the faith in the dominion of Mars? Wouldn't she find greater satisfaction and spiritual edification among the theologians of the Sun, the lovers of Venus, or even the ambitious activists of Mercury? To each of these queries her answer is a clear and definite no. And the reason for her answer is contained in a single word: Love.

"I am like the fixed center of a circle," said *Amore* to Dante in that memorable dream of the poet's early youth.[4] This image has guided us like a polestar throughout our travels with the pilgrim. It has served as an anchor for all our reflections, a compass to keep us on the straight-and-narrow path. But not until now has anyone told us quite so clearly and plainly what it really means.

In his meeting with Piccarda, Dante learns that the center of the circle is in fact the sovereign will of God. The Lord of the universe, who *is* Love Himself, has selected for each and every one of us a certain position to fill and a unique purpose to serve in His eternal plan. The love with which we love Him—the *Amore* that draws us irresistibly after any particular *image* or *reflection* of His glory—is, in the final analysis, only our acquiescence to the dictates of *His* love. Piccarda knows this. She understands that, in a profoundly important sense, "Love is fate" after all.[5]

To put it in simpler terms, Piccarda has discovered the secret of contentment. She has learned that to be successful in the quest one must be able, among other things, to recognize when it is *over*. She has realized that Love, in this context, is the capacity to *stop* at the end of the journey and *rest* in the achievement of the goal.

Naturally, this message is of particular importance to married lovers. There is great danger in the temptation to fall in love with Love itself; to assume that the quest exists simply for the thrill of questing; to forget that the object of your search stands before you in the person of your mate. Discontentment with the humble ordinariness of married life makes a husband or wife susceptible to the myth of the greener grass: the belief that greater satisfaction lies just around the bend, in yet *another* attraction, *another* conquest, *another* experience of ecstasy. Such thinking has been the undoing of many perfectly good marriages—marriages that might otherwise have become fertile ground for the growth of the Seed of Love. Francis Schaeffer explained the danger of seeking completion in human love:

> If man tries to find *everything* in a man-woman or a friend-to-friend relationship, he destroys the very thing he wants and destroys the ones he loves. He sucks them dry, he eats them up, and they as well as the relationship are destroyed. But as Christians we do not have to do that. Our sufficiency of relationship is in that which God made it to be, in the infinite-personal God, on the basis of the work of Christ in communication and love.[6]

Piccarda has found her place in Paradise, not merely in spite of, but actually in and through her imperfections and failures. With Paul, she has learned to say, "By the grace of God I am what I am" (1 Corinthians 15:10). She knows that "godliness with contentment is great gain" (1 Timothy 6:6). Married lovers can do the same by learning to "love each other's function"[7]—in other words, by recognizing and affirming the special role that God has assigned to each in the mystery of His perfect will. "Were men unfallen," writes Charles

Williams, "it is so that every romanticism would sweetly and gently enlarge; being fallen, we may still study it."[8]

It's not without reason that Dante, having learned this vital lesson, finds Beatrice more radiantly lovely than ever before.

Her beauty will only increase from this point forward.

<u>REFLECTION</u>

*There is a place where yearnings
must be swallowed up in Love.*

UPSIDE DOWN AND INSIDE OUT

'E io a lei: «Se 'l mondo fosse posto
con l'ordine ch'io veggio in quelle rote,
sazio m'avrebbe ciò che m'è proposto;
ma nel mondo sensibile si puote
veder le volte tanto più divine,
quant' elle son dal centro più remote.»

"If manifested in these circles were
The cosmic order of the universe,
I should be well content," I answered her;
"But in the world below it's the reverse."

—

Paradise, canto XXVIII, 46–49; trans. Dorothy Sayers

FROM THE MOON Dante and Beatrice shot upward into the heaven of Mercury, where bright and eager souls told earnest tales of love marred only by hopes of personal glory. Then it was on to Venus, the sphere of *Amore*, where passionate spirits spoke of reason and moderation as the only reliable safeguards of expansive and generous hearts. Scholars and divines filled the blazing circle of the Sun. Fiery heroes of faith traversed Mars's lofty dome. David, Hezekiah, and a company of the world's wisest kings basked in the silvery glow of Jupiter's domain. And in the golden sphere of Saturn, champions of prayer rose in a whirlwind of contemplative bliss to their home among the stars.

Dante and Beatrice followed them, the poet drawn irresistibly by the beauty of his guide's lovely face. Up and up they soared, arriving in the heaven of the Fixed Stars in time to glimpse the Savior Himself disappearing aloft in the midst of an angelic entourage. Looking down, Dante saw the earth, small and round, like a sand dollar at the bottom of the world's deepest sea. Dizzy with a sense of impossible height, he clutched his lady's sleeve like a frightened child.

She, of course, did not fail to comfort him; and he remained in the sphere of the stars until the apostles Peter, James, and John had tested him in the virtues of Faith, Hope, and Love. Then once more he was rocketing skyward, snatched up and carried along by the irresistible power emanating from Beatrice's laughing green eyes.

"Look down again!" shouted Beatrice. "See how far you have come!"

He obeyed; and what he saw this time nearly took his breath away. It was as if the whole of human history and human endeavor lay at his feet, paltry, puny, and vain.

In the next instant they had arrived in the *Primum Mobile*,[1] the last, highest, and most swiftly revolving of all the heavenly spheres. Gazing helplessly into the shining eyes of Beatrice, he saw reflected there—just as he had seen in the image of the double-natured gryphon—what appeared to be a minute spot of flame.

Turning to test the truth of what he saw, he beheld in the space before him a blindingly radiant point of light, infinitely small and infinitely bright. Around it, like a flaming halo, whirled a tiny ring of fire, so swift in its revolutions that the pilgrim's eyes could not trace the speed of its motion. About that ring spun another, and then another—nine fiery circles in all, each larger and slower than the one it contained.

"It is a picture," Beatrice explained in response to his bewildered stare, "of the Truth behind all truths. On that point of light depend all of nature and reality. The spark sets the inmost circle spinning by virtue of pure, undiluted Love. In the same way, the inmost ring propels the second, and the second, the third. And so on to the periphery."

"But I don't understand!" he protested. "It's exactly the opposite of the way things really are! In the real world the earth lies at the center. The model is backwards!"

She smiled. "I suppose that all depends on what you mean *by the real world*," she said. "Don't you think?"

"I tripped on my shoelace and I fell *up*," writes poet Shel Silverstein.[2]

It's in just this way—by *falling up*—that Dante and Beatrice make their ascent from the lowest to the highest of the heavenly spheres.

There's a reason our poet has chosen to employ this kind of imagery. He believes that Love is a strange, irresistible, almost inexplicable force: something like the law of gravity in reverse. He understands that once this redemptive force sets its "deeper magic" in motion, Death itself starts working backwards.[3] As a result, he's convinced that there's only one thing that can happen to a lover who escapes his personal Hell and leaves his burdens on the Mount of Reconciliation: *he flies*. Free of the weights and obstacles of sin and self, he rises like a rocket. He soars, naturally and of his own accord, to that "predestined place" prepared for him in the sovereign plan of God, "propelled there by the power of that bow which always shoots straight to its Happy Mark."[4]

And what does he discover when he reaches that celestial

spot? This is where Dante's narrative takes what may be the most surprising and dramatic twist of all; for the lesson awaiting the pilgrim at the conclusion of his long journey is that *the end is the beginning*. When Dante fell in love with Beatrice, he *fell up*; and having fallen all the way from the core to the periphery of the medieval cosmos, he finds himself, in a certain sense, right back where he started. To put it another way, his pilgrimage concludes in a world turned upside down and inside out.

In this topsy-turvy place, he learns that the center of Love's circle, the goal he has pursued so long, is located *not* at the heart of his former paltry life, but at the outermost edge of all things. In the brilliant spark of light that shines before his eyes in the *Primum Mobile* he sees an image of the God who is not merely the focal point of the universe, but "a circle whose center is everywhere and whose circumference is nowhere."[5] This God, he now perceives, is not just Love Himself but "the Alpha and the Omega, the Beginning and the End" (Revelation 1:8), the One who travels beside us in *all* our loves from start to finish. We cannot escape Him no matter where we go (Psalm 139:7). And where He is, the potential for new creation, new life, and new love is an ever-present reality (2 Corinthians 5:17).

This stunning vision is pregnant with implications for earthbound pilgrims still in the early days of our apprenticeship to *Amore*. It redefines for us the very meaning of romance. It makes Love the centerpiece of an upside-down world where the first are last and the last are first (Mark 10:31); where dying is living (John 12:25) and giving is receiving (Luke 6:38); where it is clearly seen that Love "does not seek its own" (1 Corinthians 13:5), but that serious lovers are the sort of people who prefer one another in honor and esteem (Romans 12:10; Philippians 2:3).

And that's not all. The vision of the fiery circles tells us something more as well. It says that the contentment of Piccarda, far from being the end of the story, is merely a platform from which *Amore* can launch itself again and again in a never-ending, upwardly soaring, outwardly spiraling adventure of fresh discovery and deeper intimacy. It explains why Love is eternal (1 Corinthians 13:8), why the flame of passion does not have to fade when the quest is achieved, and why the Romantic Vision need not die when lovers marry. It disperses the myth that Paradise is a place devoid of dynamism: nothing but harps and clouds and choruses of praise.

In *Manalive*, one of the wildest and most delightful of his many unconventional works of fiction, author G. K. Chesterton imagines what a vibrantly *vital* human being might be like: a man gloriously in touch with the miracle of life itself. His portrait of the eccentric Innocent Smith[6] is a picture of an individual for whom human existence is a process of perpetual rediscovery. Interestingly, this concept gets applied in a special way to the protagonist's marriage and love life. So intensely does Smith love his wife that he actually *leaves* her. Why? He wants to know the joy of *finding* her again. He sets off on a trek around the globe in order that he might wind up right back where he started: at home in his own house, more deeply in love than ever with the woman of his dreams.

> I am going to turn the world upside down, too. I'm going to turn myself upside down. I'm going to walk upside down in the cursed upsidedownland of the Antipodes, where trees and men hang head downward

in the sky. But my revolution . . . will end up in the holy, happy place—the celestial, incredible place—the place where we were before.[7]

It's with the same goal in mind that Smith develops an unusual way of spending his vacations: he leaves his wife "at schools, boarding-houses, and places of business, so that he might recover her again and again with a raid and a romantic elopement."[8]

Though his methods are hilariously unorthodox—and something less than commendable—Innocent Smith has clearly discovered a valuable secret. He has devised endless ways of renewing, repeating, and revisiting the ecstatic experience of falling in love with his wife. He has found out that the end of the quest can be a place of perpetual new beginnings. In short, he has learned how vital it is to see his wife again and again just as he saw her at the moment of their very first meeting—as Dante saw Beatrice on the streets of Florence. It's a secret that every couple desperately needs to discover.

"The way up is the way down," wrote the poet T. S. Eliot. "The way forward is the way back."[9] That's how Dante's quest began in the opening canto of *The Inferno*. What the pilgrim did not realize at that time was that this topsy-turvy path was to be his lot from that moment on—the end as well as the starting point of his journey.

He could never have imagined that it would also prove to be the key to eternal bliss.

REFLECTION

True Love springs eternal.

THE CENTER OF THE CIRCLE

Ma già volgeva il mio disio e 'l velle,
sì come rota ch'igualmente e mossa,
l'amor che move il sole e l'altre stelle.

Like a wheel in perfect balance turning,
I felt my will and my desire impelled
by the Love that moves the sun and the other stars.

—

Paradise, canto XXXIII, 143–145; trans. Mark Musa

SLOWLY THE BRILLIANT point of light faded. The encircling rings of fire sputtered and went out. In the ensuing stillness Dante found himself confronted with a vision of his lady's beauty more staggering than anything he had yet imagined.

"We have risen from the last and greatest sphere into the Empyrean," she said as he turned to face her. "This is the dwelling place of the Divine Presence. Look closely. Tell me what you see."

A silent but blinding explosion of luminescence followed. He rubbed his eyes and stared.

"A river!" he said. "A river of light! Wide and rolling, shooting out sparks, flowing grandly between banks of gold and scarlet flowers!"

"Your vision is good!" she laughed. "Now bend and drink. With your *eyes*."

He obeyed; and as he straightened up, the stream became a shining lake—an expansive luminous circle reflected on the convex surface of the *Primum Mobile*. Slowly the circle folded itself upward into the shape of a vast White Rose, its snowy petals the tiers of a celestial amphitheater wherein were enthroned all the souls of the redeemed—everyone from Adam and Eve to Peter, James, and John. At the top of the highest tier sat Mary, the mother of Jesus, like a queen in the midst of her court. Around her feet were gathered all those fair and blessed women who had conspired with Beatrice to draw the pilgrim up from the depths of Hell.

Trembling with joy, Dante turned again to seek his lady's face. But instead of Beatrice he saw standing before him an ancient man clad in the white robes of Heaven.

"Where is she?" the distraught pilgrim cried. "Where has my Beatrice gone?"

In answer, the elder pointed up to the third row of the heavenly stadium. There, amidst the queen's ladies-in-waiting, sat Beatrice herself, bright, clear, and distant as the morning star. She inclined her head to him and smiled; then turned to face the fountain of eternal light and life.

"Her task is complete," said the old man. "She sent me to guide you to the end and goal of your desire. I am Bernard of Clairvaux, devoted lover and vassal of the greatest of ladies. Lift up your eyes. Let them rise from the beauty of Beatrice to the face of the mother of our Lord. From there it is but a short step to the Vision above all visions. Look and see!"

Fixing his attention first upon the jeweled tiara that sparkled like a diamond upon the head of Beatrice, Dante allowed his gaze to slip higher until it found the shining eyes of the bearer of the Son of God. Mary too smiled and nodded; then signaled with a slight lift of her brow that he was to let his glance rise even higher. In the next instant he was staring straight into the Source of all splendor and glory: a brilliance beside which the sun itself would have appeared as darkness. With a cry of pain and ecstasy he reached for Bernard; but the old man had gone, leaving him alone with the unspeakable vision.

Dante was never afterward able to describe that vision to his own satisfaction. The impression it left upon his senses was that of a great iridescent circle. As he watched, this circle somehow resolved itself into three—three separate circles of three pure and distinct colors pulsating and revolving within the space of one. The second was like a reflection of the first. The third appeared to be breathed forth equally and simultaneously by the other two.

Like a man in a trance, the pilgrim gazed and gazed until he saw, contained within the second circle, the shape of a human face: the face of a man, gentle yet strong, with eyes that pierced to the depths of the soul.

"O Lord Christ!" he exclaimed—for he knew whose face it was—"What place does our human image have within the center of this glorious sphere? How can man be contained in God and God in man? Show me the deeper meaning of this mystery!"

With that, his mind was flooded with light from beyond the borders of understanding. Words failed and pictures faded. Poetic images dissolved and fled.

Then he surrendered himself, body and soul, to the Love that glows at the center of all things.

Every journey has an end. Every circle turns upon a center point. And every love, however great, must eventually be swallowed up in a greater one.

Dante's pilgrimage concludes as it began: with the image of the Circle. "I am as the center of a circle," said *Amore* to the young romantic in the early chapters of *La Vita Nuova*, "a circle to which all parts of the circumference are equal; but with you it is not so." *The Divine Comedy* is the story of the reversal of that sentence of judgment. It narrates in detail the poet's long journey to the center of the circle of love.

The final lines of the *Paradiso* are marked by an atmosphere of ineffable wonder and inexpressible joy. Dante spends more time professing the inadequacy of his powers of description than in telling us exactly what he saw. But this much he makes clear: when the Beatific Vision comes, it comes in the form of a circle: three great circles in one, and in the midst of the second of these a human face. It's a poetic picture of the Trinity; and, significantly, it dwells with special emphasis upon the incarnation of the second person: Jesus Christ, Son of God and Son of Man.

Who guides Dante to the point of receiving this revelation? His beloved Beatrice, the bright-eyed Florentine girl. Who conducts him to the threshold of the ultimate spiritual ecstasy? Bernard of Clairvaux, apostle of passion and composer of eighty-six sermons on the most sublime of all romantic love poems, Solomon's Song.[1] Who is on hand to witness the consummation of his bliss? Mary, Rachel, Rebecca, Lucia—in a word, all the representatives of feminine beauty and grace that heaven can muster for the occasion. It is at the encouragement of *their* nods and smiles and flashing eyes— the universal language of *Amore*—that the poet takes his final steps into the divine presence.

What does all this mean? For answers, we'll have to go back to the beginning; not merely the beginning of Dante's trek through the afterworld, but the beginning of Creation itself:

> Have you not read that He who made them at the
> beginning "made them male and female," and
> said, "For this reason a man shall leave his father
> and mother and be joined to his wife, and the two
> shall become one flesh"? (Matthew 19:4-5; quoting
> Genesis 1:27 and 2:24)

Male and female. Two in one. Herein lies the goal of
Romantic Love between a woman and a man. This is the
fulfillment of *Amore's* outward-bound quest. But it is something more as well. As Dante discovers during the last
moments of his sojourn in Paradise, it is also the essence of
the life that pulses at the heart of the universe. It is, in fact,
the principle that defines the person of Jesus Christ Himself,
"perfect God and perfect man, of a rational soul and human
flesh subsisting."[2] It's the truth Dante saw embodied in the
"twy-formed," dual-natured gryphon, as reflected in the eyes
of Beatrice at the top of Mount Purgatory: the miracle of *two
made one.*

This is the destination toward which our steps are unwit-
tingly directed when first we fall under the irresistible spell
of love between the sexes. In seeking to be joined one with
another, men and women are in actuality expressing an innate
desire to partake of the life of the Trinity: three in one, one in
three, and at the heart of the three the incomprehensible mystery of the two: spirit with flesh, and God with man, blended
like husband and wife in the bonds of matrimony.

"For we are members of His body," writes the apostle Paul,
"of His flesh and of His bones. 'For this reason a man shall
leave his father and mother and be joined to his wife, and the
two shall become one flesh.' This is a great mystery, but I speak
concerning Christ and the church" (Ephesians 5:30-32).

Charles Williams calls this the mystery of co-inherence: the marvel of me in you and you in me. The French troubadour Foulquet of Marseilles was thinking of it when he told Dante, "I would not wait for you to ask [any questions] of me were I to *inyou* as you now *inme*."[3] Jesus spoke of it, too, when He offered this prayer on His disciples' behalf:

> I do not pray for these alone, but also for those who
> will believe in Me through their word; that they all may
> be one, as You, Father, are in Me, and I in You; that
> they also may be one in Us. . . . I in them, and You in
> Me; that they may be made perfect in one, and that
> the world may know that You have sent Me, and have
> loved them as You have loved Me. (John 17:20-21, 23)

Co-inherence. Two-in-oneness. It is precisely in this way that a love affair grows into a genuine marriage, and a genuine marriage is transformed into a veritable way of the soul—an avenue of approach to the meaning of life itself, a meaning that can only be experienced in intimate relationship with one another and with the Creator of our souls. This is why it is no blasphemy to assert that, in Romantic Love, the Holy Spirit can actually reveal "the Christ-hood of two individuals to each other."[4]

Dante's story draws to a close, then, with "all the images . . . moving sweetly and strongly into God."[5] Beatrice and Florence; Virgil and Bernard; Lucia, Piccarda, and Mary; the vision of the great White Rose, medieval symbol of Romance and Courtly Love;[6] the smiles of the heavenly ladies. "These images are never quite separated, even in the beginning," notes Williams. "Towards the end they mingle and become a great complex image. They end with the inGodding of man."[7]

O Light Eternal fixed in Itself alone,
by Itself alone understood, which from Itself
loves and glows, self-knowing and self-known.[8]

This is the Love that burns at the center of the Circle. It is the Reality of which every love affair is but a rudimentary reflection. For Dante it began with a vision of a girl and ended with the vision of God. It can take us to the same destination if we will remain true to the course of Love's original trajectory.

That's because *Amore*, like every good gift that comes down from the Father of lights, finds its ultimate meaning and fulfillment only in Jesus Christ our Lord. For He is Himself the summation of *all* things, whether in heaven or on earth (Colossians 1:19; 3:11); and it is only in Him that *our* love can be caught up into "the Love that moves the sun and other stars."[9]

REFLECTION

God is Love, Christ is God, and the end
of all Love is God in Christ.

GETTING PERSONAL
When Love Seeks Fulfillment

"I NOW PRONOUNCE YOU husband and wife."

She had dreamed of hearing those words since the days of dress-up tea parties and Barbie doll games; imagined marrying a handsome prince since her daddy first called her "my little princess."

He had longed to kiss a pretty girl since the days of kindergarten cooties; tried to imagine guilt-free intimacy since ogling dirty pictures in his sixth-grade buddy's borrowed magazine.

As they enter the honeymoon, both will begin to learn just how beautifully intense and ultimately fulfilling love can be. The imaginings of fairy-tale stories and biblical admonitions will pale in comparison to the flesh-and-blood realities of marital bliss.

She will thrill when he eagerly caresses her femininity, and she will begin to know how much she is desired and cherished.

He will savor the allure of her unveiled beauty and discover the intended object and life-giving purpose of long-restrained appetites.

Each will begin saving the other from isolation's ache and experiencing the kind of rest only available to one who willingly completes another.

Nothing comes closer to the outskirts of a place known as Paradise than young virgins on their honeymoon. But as Dante discovered, the couple has a lot of work ahead before either reaches the uppermost heights of love's potential joys. Karen Carpenter got it right when she sang, "We've only just begun."

Marriage is anything but "settling down." Saying "I do" does not signal a dream come true, but rather a path made clear.

No matter where you find yourself on that path—dating a special someone with whom you hope to share your life or celebrating thirty years of marriage—much can be learned from Dante's imaginative trek up the slope of Purgatory and ascent into the light of Paradise. His admonition? If you are willing to work at it, you can become capable of giving, and in the process receiving, God-like love.

QUESTION 1: DO YOU RECOGNIZE YOURSELF AS INCOMPLETE?
If hammers had feelings, they would pine for nails. That's because hammers are made to play a purposeful role in the hand of a creative carpenter. Without nails, however, hammers can only demolish or destroy. In like manner, nails hold nothing in place until driven into the wood. And they can't drive themselves.

Like many objects in our world, each of us needs a partner to discover and fulfill the ultimate purpose for which we were created. Do you remember what God said after breathing His breath into Adam? "It is not good that man should be alone" (Genesis 2:18). Despite making man in His own image, the Lord described a solitary Adam as "not good." Not because Adam was bad. He was just incomplete, unfinished.

Perhaps the greatest mystery in Christian doctrine is that we serve one God in three distinct persons: Father, Son, and Holy Spirit. God is no lone ranger. Relationship between and within the Trinity is at the core of His essence. So it should not surprise us that no individual, not even Adam, can fully fulfill his or her purpose of reflecting the image of God. That's why God made "a helper comparable to" Adam and hard-wired both men and women to "become one flesh." In short, solitude is not good because it is not like God.

Every one of us was made for emotional and physical intimacy with others—first and foremost, a husband or wife. So those who are single should let their ache for intimacy with a special someone remind them that we are gloriously incomplete, made to be given to another in the bond of holy matrimony or to "marry" Christ through lifelong celibate service.

Those of us who are married must continually push past the tendency to withdraw, protect, or isolate ourselves. We need to let the beloved person God has placed in our lives complete us. We should allow his or her hammer to give purpose to our nail.

What purpose? According to one ancient church council:

The sacrament of Matrimony signifies the union of Christ and the Church. It gives spouses the grace to love each other with the love with which Christ has loved his Church; the grace of the sacrament thus perfects the human love of the spouses, strengthens

their indissoluble unity, and sanctifies them on the
way to eternal life.[1]

In other words, the ups and downs of marital love are
intended to conform us more and more to the image of a
God of Love, a God of relationship, and a God we were
made to reflect.

QUESTION 2: HAVE YOU MADE YOUR SEXUALITY AN ICON OR AN IDOL?

Do you know the difference between an icon and an idol?

Icons are images that reflect and point to a greater reality. On your computer screen, an icon provides a visual representation of a software program. The icon's only power is
to remind you and connect you. In like manner, religious
icons provide worshipers with tangible reminders of Christ
or departed saints—a bit like the ink on the pages of a Bible.
As important as the ink on the page may be, Christians do
not worship the typeset words "Jesus is Lord." We worship
the person those words describe. Iconic images, like printed
words, *connect* us to the reality of the living, invisible God.

Idols, by contrast, *replace* God as the object of our worship. They point only to themselves. Rather than inciting
humility before the unseen God, they serve an insidious process the apostle Paul described in his letter to the church at
Rome:

Although they knew God, they did not glorify Him
as God, nor were thankful, but became futile in their
thoughts, and their foolish hearts were darkened.
Professing to be wise, they became fools, and changed

the glory of the incorruptible God into an image made like corruptible man—and birds and four-footed animals and creeping things. Therefore God also gave them up to uncleanness, in the lusts of their hearts, to dishonor their bodies among themselves, who exchanged the truth of God for the lie, and worshiped and served the creature rather than the Creator, who is blessed forever. Amen. (Romans 1:21-25)

Paul goes on to describe increasingly perverse sexual obsession and deviance among those who worshiped idols. The connection to Dante's romantic journey couldn't be more direct. God made human sexuality and romantic attraction as an icon of His own image and intended relationship between God and mankind. That is why so much biblical imagery is centered around the "icon" of marriage. Throughout the Old Testament, Israel is described as God's unfaithful wife. The New Testament describes the church as the bride of Christ—and ends with God and mankind united in eternal bliss following a marriage supper. Paul later describes what this icon is intended to reflect in his letter to the church at Ephesus. "For this reason a man shall leave his father and mother and be joined to his wife, and the two shall become one flesh." What reason? "This is a great mystery, but I speak concerning Christ and the church" (Ephesians 5:31-32).

When we understand our union with the opposite sex as an icon reflecting God's relationship with His beloved, it drives us further toward the beatific vision of pure, intense, inexpressible love. It is no stretch to recognize the climax of sexual union between husband and wife as a faint picture of and connection to the kind of mutually fulfilling intimacy each of us was made to know. Maybe that's why traditional wedding vows use the phrase "With my body I thee worship."

When we make sexual union an idol, on the other hand, it drives us further and further away from what we were made to be and whom we were made to reflect. Sexuality becomes about self-centered taking rather than self-sacrificial giving. Intimacy becomes a means to personal gratification instead of mutual satisfaction. In short, something beautiful becomes ugly and dehumanizing.

Christopher West said it best. "If we want to know what's most sacred in this world, all we need do is look for what is most violently profaned."[2]

So which will it be for you? A sacred icon or a profane idol?

QUESTION 3: ARE YOU WATCHING YOUR STEPS?

From his first steps down Inferno's descending path to his ascension up Mount Purgatory into Paradise, Dante encountered one reminder after another that the romantic journey is a perilous quest. To negotiate a narrow path on a steep slope one needs sure footing to avoid sliding backward or stumbling down the ravine.

The upward path of physical attraction, for example, is intended to lead us to the beauty and meaning only marriage and parenthood can bring. Its downward slope, on the other hand, can drag us toward dehumanizing acts of obsession and abuse.

As souls littered across Dante's journey revealed, each of us leans toward a slightly different pitfall. What is yours? Where should you be minding your steps as you pursue Love's call?

Do you know yourself vulnerable to lusts that steal away

the pure joy available through fidelity? What must you do to climb rather than descend?

Are you prone to isolation, defending yourself from happiness by pushing others away? What can you do to move out of your lonely comfort zone?

Are you too proud to apologize?

Have you made yourself the idol of your own life rather than the icon of His?

Do you find yourself prone to greed rather than giving, anger rather than patience, gluttony instead of temperance, or sloth over diligence? If so, you climb the same path as the rest of humanity.

One or more of these deadly propensities will kill the hope of intimacy with God and others. The daily irritations and opportunities that surface in your marriage or love relationship can drive growth and maturity or tragic descent. Which will it be for you?

And so we come full circle to the fundamental truth of our existence. As those created in God's image, we are hardwired for a love that finds its source and aim in Him. We fully live only when we fully love. And we fully love only when we, like Christ, give ourselves away.

> Beloved, if God so loved us, we also ought to love
> one another. No one has seen God at any time. If
> we love one another, God abides in us, and His love
> has been perfected in us. . . . God is love, and he
> who abides in love abides in God, and God in him.
> (1 John 4:11-12, 16)

AFTERTHOUGHTS

Romance and the Christian Imagination

. . . only a shell, a husk of meaning,
From which the purpose breaks only when it is fulfilled.

—

T. S. Eliot, Four Quartets

As AN EARNEST young believer caught up in the fires of the Jesus Movement of the early 1970s, my wife received a special gift from an equally fervent young Christian friend: a small, enameled cross bearing a brightly painted image of the tree of life. I remember how she loved that little cross. She wore it everywhere. For weeks no one ever saw her without it. She was heartbroken when it suddenly turned up missing.

That friend had an explanation for this disappointing turn of events. "You obviously loved it too much," she said, "so the Lord took it away. Our God is a jealous God. He doesn't want *anything* usurping His place in our affections. Natural loves can't be allowed to stand in the way. Jesus comes first."

This was a bit hard to swallow. Yes, she had loved the cross, but not for its own sake. She had loved it because it *meant* something. For her, it symbolized and embodied important transcendent realities: friendship, generosity, beauty, grace. It wasn't just a piece of remarkable craftsman-ship—it was a striking and intensely personal reminder of the life-giving love of a dying Savior. As such, it had a way of turning her thoughts toward heaven. She knew intuitively that the reasons for her attachment to it were anything but blameworthy. But she wasn't able to verbalize any of this at the time.

So she received her friend's reproach without a word of protest.

Too Much Love?

Somehow this incident came to mind as I was pondering the closing scene of Dante's *Divine Comedy*—the one in which, according to Charles Williams, "all the images are moving sweetly and strongly into God."[1] As I mulled it over, I was struck again with the thought that it was in fact Dante's fierce attachment to a "natural love"—his fascination with a vis-ible, earthly, and human reflection of the divine goodness and grace—that led him at last to the consummation of his spiri-tual pilgrimage.

I remembered, too, the rebuke he had received from his lover at the top of Mount Purgatory, and I saw how differ-ent it was from the reproof of my wife's youthful friend. For Beatrice never accused Dante of loving her *too much*. She never said that God had taken her away in order to punish the poet for his idolizing devotion. On the contrary, she faulted him for his faithlessness. She told him in effect that *he hadn't loved her enough*. She insisted that even after her death he should have remained true to her memory by clinging to the *eternal* significance of her "buried flesh." Only by taking her exhortation to heart was he able to redirect his footsteps to heaven.

There can be no mistaking the central message of this story. *Genuine love is something of which we can never have too much.* As long as it is pure, as long as its trajectory remains straight and true, love must eventually lead us aright. If it is clean, wholesome, appropriate, and selfless, then a passion for something or someone other than ourselves inevitably carries about it a certain aura of holiness. It always represents a step, however feeble and small, in the direction of the Great Lover of our souls.

Images Rejected . . . and Affirmed

To state the same principle in different terms, Dante tells us that there is a definite place for images in the life of Christian devotion. That is to say, he asserts the value of the imagination—the image-making and image-embracing faculty of the human psyche. He agrees with A. W. Tozer that, when it comes to our relationship with God, "we learn by using what we already know as a bridge over which we pass to the unknown."[2] In so doing, he places himself squarely on one side of a debate that has been raging almost since the beginning of church history, a controversy between the adherents of two divergent pathways of spiritual growth and progress: what Charles Williams calls the way of "the Rejection of Images" and the way of "the Affirmation of Images."[3]

My wife's friend was a firm believer in the pathway of Rejection. Fearful of loving anything more than she loved God, she fastidiously observed the Old Testament proscription against "any graven image, or any likeness" (Exodus 20:4, KJV). Like Ulrich Zwingli, the stern Swiss Reformer, she was an iconoclast—an unrelenting smasher of "religious" symbols. Like the author of *The Cloud of Unknowing*, the great classic of medieval mysticism, she was convinced that the secret of Christian perfection is to "hate to think of anything but God Himself," to "try to forget all created things that He ever made . . . so that your thought and longing do not reach out to them."[4] Like the psalmist, she was painfully anxious to be able to say, "Whom have I in heaven but You? And there is none upon earth that I desire besides You" (Psalm 73:25).

Many great believers have followed this road: Gideon, Elijah, St. Anthony of the desert, Francis of Assisi, Augustine of Hippo, John Calvin, and John Knox. So far as it goes, it is a time-honored and perfectly legitimate method of pursuing purity of heart. But there is another way.

The Eye of the Beholder

The lamp of the body is the eye. Therefore, when your eye is good, your whole body also is full of light. But when your eye is bad, your body also is full of darkness. (Luke 11:34)

With these words, Jesus does more than acknowledge the impact of visual imagery upon the human spirit. He also suggests that such imagery is virtually inescapable. We can't avoid looking at the world and seeing the many attractive things with which it is filled. Nor can we fully prevent our "thought and longing"—our imagination—from "reach[ing] out to them." The way of Rejection, then, is exceedingly difficult to follow. But the path of Affirmation lies open to all who are capable of understanding that, ultimately, good and evil reside not in the image but in the eye. It's *how* we look and *how* we see that makes all the difference.

This is precisely the lesson Dante learns during the course of his trek through the circles, terraces, and spheres of the afterlife. The eye that insists on looking with selfishness, lust, or greed must descend with Francesca, Brunetto, and Geryon into the realms of infernal darkness. But the eye that is practiced to discern the invisible attributes of the unseen God in the tangible things He has made (Romans 1:20)—*that* eye will eventually pierce the mysteries of the Kingdom of glory. This is why our poet can refer to his Florentine girl as a ray of human "sunlight."[5] This is how he is able to speak of his eyes as "the gates she entered with the fire that burns me still."[6]

Man: The Image of God

The images to which the imagination can fasten itself are virtually unlimited in number and kind. They can assume the shape of a good daydream or an oft-told tale. They can jump out at us from Beethoven's *Moonlight Sonata*, Keats's *Ode on a Grecian Urn*, or Van Gogh's *Starry Night*. Sometimes they flash like lightning across the heavens. On other occasions they creep silently out of the smallest and most secret corners of the mind. Any one of them—a windswept moon or an evening of rain, a dim childhood memory or a twinge of homesickness—can become a reflection, a hint, a suggestion of Something beyond itself. Any one of them may represent an invitation to an encounter with the God who alone can address the deepest longings of the heart.

And yet, for all that, there is good reason for the scriptural prohibition of "likenesses." For the imagination, like the rest of human nature, is easily led astray. It quickly forgets that the meaning of the universe is wrapped up not in the material stuff of which the world is made—gems and stars, houses and lands, the words of the poets or the tresses of a fresh young girl—but in *personality*. It loses sight of the fact that you and

I are designed to find our destiny within the context of an I-Thou relationship.

To put it another way, the Bible forbids man-made representations of the deity for the simple reason that they are superfluous. They are superfluous because God has *already given* us a picture of Himself—*in one another* (Matthew 25:37-40). "God created man *as* His image," says the Hebrew text of Genesis 1:27, "*as* the image of God created He him."[7] Translated in this way, the familiar passage becomes a strikingly bold assertion. It makes the shocking claim that man himself *is* a copy or a graphic image of the Creator—a formal, visible, and understandable representation of who God is and what He is really like.

Man as Male and Female

This biblical teaching has profound and far-reaching implications. It explains why the image to which the human imagination most naturally and readily gravitates is that of *another person*. It reveals why the soul of every landscape is a story and the heart of every story a human character. It illuminates the reason for the timeless appeal of the most winsome and popular stories of all—tales of love and romance. For while the nature of God can be perceived in *any* interpersonal relationship, the fact remains that the light of divine *Agape* is reflected with unique brilliance in the mirror of human *Amore*: the mature love of a man for a woman and a woman for a man.

This is not just Dante's idea. It is a recurrent scriptural theme. We find it in Solomon's passion for the Shulamite woman and Hosea's pursuit of the faithless Gomer. It shows up in the language of the prophets, who love to portray Yahweh as a possessive husband and Israel as His wandering bride. It confronts us in Paul's description of marriage as a transcendent mystery, an icon of Christ's relationship with His church. It is the basis for Revelation's depiction of the celestial wedding feast.

Ultimately, it all goes back to the *imago dei*—the image of God in man. "God created man as His own image," says Genesis, "as the image of God He created him"; and then, significantly, the text adds, "*male and female He created them*" (emphasis added). Here, too, is a tremendous mystery. For what these words seem to suggest is that, in some way we cannot completely grasp or explain, God's self-portrait comes through most clearly in the maleness and femaleness of humankind. It receives its fullest expression in the division of the sexes and in their quest for complement, reunion, and fulfillment in marriage and romantic love.

The End . . . and the Beginning

I suppose this is the real reason my wife and her little enameled cross rose up before my mind's eye when I began looking for a way to bring our travels with Dante to a meaningful conclusion. I wasn't really thinking about what the cross had meant to Joni. I was realizing what Joni means to me. As the images of the poet's story converged—the bright smile and flashing eyes of Beatrice mingling with and superimposing themselves upon the beauty of Piccarda, the piety of Bernard, the glory of the Celestial Rose, and the brilliance of the concentric circles of light—it was to be expected that another smile and another pair of eyes should thrust themselves upon my imagination. In that instant it was inevitable that my thoughts and feelings should be drawn to the one who has been for me not only friend and lover, not merely an object of passion or the goal of desire, but a tangible, embraceable, and ever-present icon of God's love embodied in human flesh.

For in the final analysis, I am not altogether unlike Dante Alighieri. I, too, saw a girl at a strategic point in life's journey. I, too, discovered in that moment what it means to be intoxicated with love, lifted out of self, taken captive by *Amore*. Though I am in many respects quite different from the medieval Italian poet, there is nevertheless this important point of similarity between us: before seeing the girl, I was in a very real sense trapped alone within the confines of an imagination too narrow to accommodate the richness of the divine imagery filling the world around me. Like Dante, I "needed a human being to launch [my] return to the land of the living."[8] I saw a girl, and for more than thirty-five years she has filled this vital role in my life. She was and is my Beatrice—the wife of my youth and the companion of my quest.

This, of course, is not the end of our story. It is just the beginning. When all is said and done, *every* image must be recognized for what it is—"only a shell, a husk of meaning." This applies to a lifelong romance as surely as it does to a lingering sunset or a haunting snatch of birdsong. The significance of such things does not lie within the things themselves. Their purpose will break forth and be revealed only when the *real* quest has been achieved. That's why what Dante called "high fantasy" must ultimately fail.[9] And that's why Joni and I will never understand the full meaning of our love for one another until it has been completely eclipsed in the glory of the Beatific Vision.

Jim Ware

ENDNOTES

Introduction: Love's Divergent Paths (Kurt Bruner)
1. "Maria," music by Leonard Bernstein, lyrics by Stephen Sondheim © 1956, 1957 Amberson Holdings LLC and Stephen Sondheim. Copyright renewed by Leonard Bernstein Music Publishing Company, publisher.
2. Christopher West, *Theology of the Body for Beginners* (West Chester, PA: Ascension Press, 2004), 25.
3. *The Catechism of the Catholic Church* (New York: Doubleday, 1995), 447.
4. *The Book of Common Prayer* (New York: Oxford University Press, 1928), 300, emphasis added.
5. C. S. Lewis, *The Screwtape Letters* (New York: Bantam Classics, 1995), 26.

Part 1: Love Kindled *(La Vita Nuova/The New Life)*
Captive
1. Dante, *La Vita Nuova*, trans. Mark Musa (Bloomington, IN: Indiana University Press, 1973), chapter III; 6.
2. Dante, *The Divine Comedy*, Vol. 2, *Purgatory* (New York: Penguin Books, 1981, 1985), canto XXIV, lines 52–54; 259.
3. Charles Williams, *The Figure of Beatrice* (Berkeley, CA: Apocryphile Press, 2005), 7.
4. Dante, *La Vita Nuova*, ed. and trans. Stanley Appelbaum (Mineola, NY: Dover Publications, 2006), 3.
5. "Beaver's Crush," *Leave It To Beaver*, Season 1, DVD (Universal Studios Home Entertainment, 2005).
6. Cf. C. S. Lewis, *The Four Loves* (San Diego: Harcourt Brace Jovanovich Publishers, 1960).
7. *The Portable Dante*, ed. Paolo Milano (New York: The Viking Press, 1947); *Paradiso* (trans. Laurence Binyon), canto XXXIII, line 145; 544.

Bereft
1. *La Vita Nuova/The New Life*, trans. Stanley Appelbaum, 69.
2. Ibid.
3. Alfred, Lord Tennyson, "In Memoriam A. H. H.", xxvii, in *Idylls of the King and a Selection of Poems* (New York: Signet Classics, 1961), 302.

4. Samuel Butler, *The Way of All Flesh* (Mineola, New York: Dover Publications, 2004), 262.
5. Sheldon Vanauken, *A Severe Mercy* (San Francisco: Harper & Row Publishers, 1977), 217.
6. Ibid., 209.
7. Ibid., 211, emphasis in original.
8. Williams, *The Figure of Beatrice*, 38.
9. *Purgatory*, trans. Mark Musa, canto XXXI, lines 47–48.

Betrayal
1. *La Vita Nuova/The New Life*, trans. Stanley Appelbaum, chapter XLII; 97.
2. Some have actually suggested that Gemma was the "Lady in the Window." See Paget Toynbee, *Dante Alighieri: His Life and Works*, 67, note 1. The marriage remained intact throughout Dante's lifetime (though in estrangement during the years of his exile) and produced four children.
3. At the time of her death, our poet's ideal woman had been married to Simone dei Bardi, a Florentine banker, for more than three years.
4. Williams, *Figure of Beatrice*, 20.
5. Charles Williams, *Religion and Love in Dante: The Theology of Romantic Love* (Westminster: Dacre Press, n.d.), 7. Rereleased by Kessinger Publishing, 2007.
6. *La Vita Nuova*, chapter XI; trans. Stanley Appelbaum.
7. Williams, *Religion and Love in Dante*, 9–10.
8. *The Divine Comedy: Hell*, trans. Dorothy Sayers (New York: Penguin Books, 1955), 95.

Part 2: Love Gone Astray *(Inferno)*
Another Way

1. Dante, *The Divine Comedy*, Vol. 1, *Inferno*, trans. Mark Musa (New York: Penguin Books, 2003), canto I, lines 77–78.
2. Ibid., lines 94–95.
3. *Purgatory*, canto XXX, lines 136–138.

Chain of Love

1. *The Inferno*, canto III, 8–9.
2. The Apostles' Creed.
3. *La Vita Nuova*, chapter XIX, trans. Dante Gabriel Rossetti; in *The Portable Dante*.
4. *Purgatory*, cantos XXVII, XXVIII, and following.
5. For this imagery, see Daniel Chanan Matt, trans., *Zohar: The Book of*

Enlightenment (Mahwah, NJ: Paulist Press, 1983), "The Birth of Moses," 100; also note, 237.

Off-Center

1. Williams, *Figure of Beatrice*, 117.
2. "Many critics, taken in like the Pilgrim by Francesca's smooth speech, have asserted that she and Paolo in their love have 'conquered' Hell because they are still together. But their togetherness is certainly part of their punishment." *Inferno*, trans. Mark Musa; canto V, notes, 118.
3. Williams, *Figure of Beatrice*, 7.
4. *Inferno*, canto V, lines 55 and 63.
5. Williams, *Figure of Beatrice*, 117.
6. Ibid., 48.
7. Ibid., 164.

Surprise, Surprise!

1. *Pirates of the Caribbean: The Curse of the Black Pearl.* Directed by Gore Verbinski; written by Ted Elliott, Terry Rossio, Stuart Beattie, and Jay Wolpert. Walt Disney Pictures, 2003.
2. *Inferno*, trans. Mark Musa, canto VI, line 81.
3. *Inferno*, trans. Dorothy Sayers, canto VI, lines 85–86.
4. Williams, *Figure of Beatrice*, 130.
5. *Inferno*, trans. Mark Musa, canto XV, lines 82–85; trans. Dorothy Sayers, 86–87.
6. T. S. Eliot, "Dante," in *The Sacred Wood: Essays on Poetry and Criticism* (1922; Great Books Online, www.bartleby.com/200/sw14/html), 4.
7. Williams, *Figure of Beatrice*, 130.
8. Quote in final sentence taken from *Inferno*, trans. Stanley Appelbaum, canto XV, line 69.

Hidden Beast

1. Paget Toynbee, *Dante Alighieri: His Life and Works* (Mineola, NY: Dover Publications, 2005), 48, footnote 1. The reference is to *Commento di Francesco da Buti sopra la Divina Commedia di Dante Alighieri*, completed 1385 and 1395, published at Pisa, 1858–1862, by Crescentino Giannini. See also *Paradise*, canto XI, line 87.
2. See *Inferno*, canto I, for the significance of the leopard.
3. It's worth adding here that Dante, by his own request, was buried in the habit of a Franciscan monk.

Final Destination

1. NBC News, "Scott Peterson Sentenced to Death," March 17, 2005, see http://www.msnbc.msn.com/id/7204523/.
2. "Little Omie Wise," trad.; as performed by Doc Watson. Based on the true

story of the murder of Naomi Wise by her lover Jonathan Lewis in Deep
River, Randolph County, NC, in 1808. Reprinted in *The Songs of Doc
Watson* (Oak Publications, 1998), 40–41. Other traditional ballads of this
type include "The Banks of the Ohio," "The Lone Green Valley," " The
Knoxville Girl," "The Wexford Girl," "The Cruel Miller," and "Down in
the Willow Garden."

3. Williams, *Figure of Beatrice*, 144.
4. C. S. Lewis, *Mere Christianity* (New York: MacMillan Publishing Company,
   1943, 1945, 1952), 49–50.
5. Williams, *Figure of Beatrice*, 142–144.

Getting Personal: When Love Goes Astray
1. C. S. Lewis, *The Great Divorce* (New York: Harper One, 2001), 96.
2. Lewis, *The Great Divorce*, 102.

Part 3: Love Fulfilled (*Purgatory* and *Paradise*)
Press On!
1. Williams, *Figure of Beatrice*, 145.
2. *Purgatory*, trans. Mark Musa, canto XVIII, lines 103–104.
3. The *canzone* is found in Book III of Dante's unfinished work, the *Convivio*.
4. *La Vita Nuova*, chapter XIX.
5. *Inferno*, trans. Mark Musa, canto III, lines 17–18.
6. Williams, *Religion and Love in Dante*, 25.

The Seed
1. *Purgatory*, trans. Mark Musa, canto XVII, lines 127–129.
2. As in the famous prayer of Augustine: "You have made us for yourself, and
   our hearts are restless until they can find peace in You." *Confessions*, I, I;
   trans. Rex Warner (New York: Mentor Books, 1963), 17.
3. Peter J. Leithart, *Ascent to Love: A Guide to Dante's Divine Comedy* (Moscow,
   ID: Canon Press, 2001), 108.
4. *Purgatory*, trans. Dorothy Sayers, canto XVIII, lines 43–45.
5. *La Vita Nuova*, canto XIX.
6. *Purgatory*, canto II, line 112.
7. Williams, *Figure of Beatrice*, 163.
8. *Purgatory*, trans. Mark Musa, canto XVIII, lines 73–75.

A Rude Welcome
1. With the exception of Sir Galahad, of course.
2. See Williams, *Figure of Beatrice*, 183.

3. Williams, *Figure of Beatrice*, 183.
4. *Purgatory*, trans. John Ciardi, canto XXXI, lines 121–123.

Contentment

1. See Williams, *Figure of Beatrice*, 96–97.
2. For a detailed and scholarly treatment of this cosmological scheme, see C. S. Lewis, *The Discarded Image* (Cambridge: Cambridge University Press, 1964).
3. Forese Donati appears on the Terrace of the Gluttons in *Purgatorio*, canto XXIII.
4. *La Vita Nuova*, canto XII.
5. Williams, *Figure of Beatrice*, 196.
6. Francis Schaeffer, *True Spirituality* (Wheaton, IL: Tyndale House Publishers, 1971), 161.
7. Williams, *Figure of Beatrice*, 195.
8. Ibid., 196.

Upside Down and Inside Out

1. *Primum Mobile* is Latin for "First Mover." As the outermost sphere of the physical cosmos, it stands closest to the *Empyrean*, the abode of God Himself. Its rapid rotation, driven by love of the Creator, sets all the other spheres in motion.
2. Shel Silverstein, "Falling Up," in *Falling Up* (New York: HarperCollins Publishers, 1996), 7.
3. See C. S. Lewis, *The Lion, The Witch and the Wardrobe* (London: Collins, 1974), 148.
4. *Paradise*, trans. Mark Musa, canto I, lines 124–126.
5. Attributed to St. Bonaventure; see Williams, *Figure of Beatrice*, 24.
6. Smith is a strangely winsome character who in some ways bears an odd resemblance to Dante. "I have become a pilgrim," he says, "to cure myself of being an exile."
7. G. K. Chesterton, *Manalive* (Mineola, NY: Dover Publications, 2000), 100.
8. Ibid., 121–122.
9. T. S. Eliot, *Four Quartets*, "The Dry Salvages," III (Orlando, FL: Harcourt, Inc., 1943, 1971), 41.

The Center of the Circle

1. Bernard of Clairvaux (1090–1153), architect of the medieval cult of the adoration of the Virgin and founder of what was perhaps the most influential new monastic order of the Middle Ages, the Cistercians, devoted eighteen years of his life to his literary masterpiece, *Sermons on the Song of Songs*. For a highly readable selection of these sermons, see *Talks on the Song of Songs*, trans. Bernard Bangley (Brewster, MA: Paraclete Press, 2002).

2. The Athanasian Creed.
3. Italian *"s'io m'intuassi, come tu t'inmii."* *Paradise*, canto IX, line 81. A literal translation of the Italian renders *inyou* and *inme* as one word each.
4. Charles Williams, *The Descent of the Dove: A Short History of the Holy Spirit in the Church* (Grand Rapids, MI: William B. Eerdmans Publishing Company, 1980), 131.
5. Williams, *Figure of Beatrice*, 97.
6. As, most notably, in Guillaume de Lorris and Jean de Meun, *The Romance of the Rose*, trans. Frances Horgan (Oxford: Oxford University Press, 1994).
7. Williams, *Figure of Beatrice*, 11.
8. *Paradise*, trans. John Ciardi, canto XXXIII, lines 124–126.
9. *Paradise*, trans. Dorothy Sayers, canto XXXIII, line 145.

Getting Personal: When Love Seeks Fulfillment
1. Council of Trent summary from *Catechism of the Catholic Church*, 463.
2. West, *Theology of the Body for Beginners*, 12.

Afterthoughts: Romance and the Christian Imagination (Jim Ware)
1. Williams, *The Figure of Beatrice*, chapter 6.
2. A. W. Tozer, *The Knowledge of the Holy* (New York: HarperCollins, 1961), 6.
3. See Williams, *The Descent of the Dove*, 129.
4. *The Cloud of Unknowing and Other Works*, trans. Clifton Wolters (New York: Penguin Books, 1961, 1978), 61.
5. *Paradise*, trans. Mark Musa, canto XXX, line 74.
6. Ibid., canto XXVI, lines 14–15.
7. See D. J. A. Clines, "The Image of God in Man," *Tyndale Bulletin* 19 (1968), 53–103. Clines argues that the Hebrew preposition *be* ("in") in the phrases *betsalmenu*, "in our image," and *betsalmo*, "in his image," should be taken as an instance of "*beth* essentiae" or "*beth* of the essence." "Thus we may say that according to Genesis 1, man does not *have* the image of God, nor is he made *in* the image of God, but is himself the image of God." Yes, that image was obscured in the Fall; however, Jesus came to earth as the perfect image of his Father. And in Christ, the blurred image of God shines out of us, his followers, as our love becomes an expression of his love.
8. Janine Langan, "The Christian Imagination," in *The Christian Imagination*, ed. Leland Ryken (Colorado Springs, CO: Shaw Books, 2002), 74.
9. *Paradise*, trans. Mark Musa, canto XXXIII, line 142.

BIBLIOGRAPHY

Editions of Dante

La Divina Commedia, Canti Scelti/The Divine Comedy, Selected Cantos. Translated by Stanley Appelbaum. Mineola, NY: Dover Publications, 2006.

The Divine Comedy. Translated by Laurence Binyon; in *The Portable Dante*. New York: The Viking Press, 1947.

The Divine Comedy. Translated by John Ciardi. New York: New American Library, 2003.

The Divine Comedy. Translated by Allen Mandelbaum. New York: Bantam Classics, 1980.

The Divine Comedy. Translated by Mark Musa. New York: Penguin Books, 1984.

The Divine Comedy. Translated by Dorothy Sayers. New York: Penguin Books, 1949.

La Vita Nuova/The New Life. Translated by Stanley Appelbaum. Mineola, NY: Dover Publications, 2006.

La Vita Nuova. Translated by Mark Musa. Bloomington, IN: Indiana University Press, 1973.

La Vita Nuova. Translated by Dante Gabriel Rossetti; in *The Portable Dante*. New York: The Viking Press, 1947.

Other Sources

Augustine. *Confessions*. Translated by Rex Warner. New York: Mentor Books, 1963.

Bernard of Clairvaux. *Talks on the Song of Songs*. Edited by Bernard Bangley. Brewster, MA: Paraclete Press, 2002.

The Book of Common Prayer. New York: Oxford University Press, 1928 Edition. Republished 2007.

Butler, Samuel. *The Way of All Flesh*. Mineola, NY: Dover Publications, 2004.

The Catechism of the Catholic Church: Second Edition. New York: Doubleday, 1995.

Chesterton, G. K. *Manalive*. Mineola, NY: Dover Publications, 2000.

Clines, D. J. A., "The Image of God in Man," *Tyndale Bulletin* 19 (1968): 53–103.

The Cloud of Unknowing and Other Works. Translated by Clifton Wolters. New York: Penguin Books, 1961, 1978.

Eliot, T. S. *Four Quartets*. Orlando, FL: Harcourt, Inc., 1943, 1971.

———. *The Sacred Wood: Essays on Poetry and Criticism*. Great Books Online (www.bartleby.com/200/sw14/html), 1922.

Leithart, Peter J. *Ascent to Love: A Guide to Dante's Divine Comedy*. Moscow, ID: Canon Press, 2001.

Lewis, C. S. *The Allegory of Love*. Oxford: Oxford University Press, 1968.

———. *The Discarded Image*. Cambridge: Cambridge University Press, 1964.

———. *The Four Loves*. San Diego, CA: Harcourt Brace Jovanovich, 1960.

———. *The Great Divorce*. New York: Harper One, 2001.

———. *The Lion, the Witch and the Wardrobe*. London: Collins, 1974.

———. *Mere Christianity*. New York: Macmillan Publishing Company, 1943.

———. *The Screwtape Letters*. New York: Bantam Classics, 1995.

Lorris, Guilliaume de, and Jean de Meun. *The Romance of the Rose*. Translated by Frances Horgan. Oxford: Oxford University Press, 1994.

Ryken, Leland, ed. *The Christian Imagination*. Colorado Springs, CO: Shaw Books, 2002.

Schaeffer, Francis A. *True Spirituality*. Wheaton, IL: Tyndale House Publishers, 1971.

Silverstein, Shel. *Falling Up*. New York: HarperCollins, 1996.

Tennyson, Alfred, Lord. *Idylls of the King and a Selection of Poems*. New York: Signet Classics, 1961.

Toynbee, Paget. *Dante Alighieri: His Life and Works*. Mineola, NY: Dover Publications, 2005.

Tozer, A. W. *The Knowledge of the Holy*. New York: HarperCollins, 1961.

Vanauken, Sheldon. *A Severe Mercy*. San Francisco: Harper & Row, 1977.

Watson, Doc. *The Songs of Doc Watson*. Oak Publications, 1998.

West, Christopher. *Theology of the Body for Beginners*. West Chester, PA: Ascension Press, 2004.

Williams, Charles. *Descent of the Dove: A Short History of the Holy Spirit in the Church*. Grand Rapids, MI: William B. Eerdmans Publishing Company, 1980.

———. *The Figure of Beatrice*. Berkeley, CA: Apocryphile Press, 2005.

———. *Religion and Love in Dante: The Theology of Romantic Love*. Westminster: Dacre Press, n.d.. Rereleased by Kessinger Publishing, 2007.

Zohar: The Book of Enlightenment. Edited and translated by Daniel Chanan Matt. Mahwah, NJ: Paulist Press, 1983.

Go deeper into these classic tales
with best-selling authors
KURT BRUNER and JIM WARE...

Finding God in The Lord of the Rings
Uncover the deep connections between Earth and Middle-earth, and let yourself be newly inspired by this tale of hope, redemption, and faith against all odds.

978-1-4143-1279-8

Finding God in The Hobbit
Jim Ware reveals the latent themes of virtue, salvation, and God's sovereignty that underscore Tolkien's original fantasy of Middle-earth.

978-1-4143-0596-7

Finding God in the Land of Narnia
Discover the deep spiritual themes of redemption and grace found in the popular Chronicles of Narnia series by C. S. Lewis.

978-0-8423-8104-8